Wisdom

Practical Answers to Today's Problems From the Proverbs

by

Dr. Jerry Kirchner

Published by:

The McDougal Publishing Co.
P.O. Box 3595
Hagerstown, MD   21742-3595

ISBN 1-884369-43-X

Printed in the United States of America
For Worldwide Distribution

Contents

1. The Value of Wisdom 13
2. The Fear of the Lord 27
3. The Need to Be Teachable 45
4. Learning to Trust in God 61
5. The Nature of the Sinner 73
6. Wisdom In Raising Children 85
7. Righteous Living 97
8. True and False Riches 111
9. The Benefits of a Generous Spirit 123
10. The Power of the Tongue 135
11. Learning to Avoid Anger 147
12. Striving for Maturity 155

Other Books by Dr. Kirchner:

The Master Calls *
A Place By Me *
Let the Oppressed Go Free *
Learn God's Word, Receive His Rewards *
Hanging By A Thread

*also available in Chinese

Author's Foreword

The Book of Proverbs is often referred to as a book of wisdom. I believe this portion of the sacred Scriptures contains much that is crucial to believers. As we feast on the truths of this wonderful book, we will grow in wisdom and understanding.

There are thirty-one chapters in the book of Proverbs and, as there are thirty or thirty-one days in most months, this book is very practical as a daily meditation — for individuals or for groups. It has something for every day and something for every member of the family. Proverbs is a book to live by.

If families could read together one chapter of Proverbs each day, it would go a long way toward alleviating the lack of moral and spiritual preparedness we face in our society. The wisdom of this book is guaranteed to change the life of anyone willing to submit himself to it. God's wisdom, properly applied to our lives, will make us successful in whatever we do.

The important themes of Proverbs are repeated throughout the book. Just as advertising agencies have learned to repeat certain phrases until they are sealed into our collective memory, God's Word repeats phrases that are important to our development. Get them into your spirit, and they will help you to face life's difficult situations.

Solomon is believed to have been the author of most of the book of Proverbs, but there are apparently contributions from other wise men as well. Solomon may have been the wisest man who ever lived, but he was not the only wise man. Indeed, God has offered His wisdom to every believer. He has promised:

> *If any of you lack wisdom, let him ask of God, that giveth to all men liberally, and upbraideth not; and it shall be given him.*   James 1:5

Certainly we could all use an extra dose of wisdom. None of us has enough and to spare. *"It shall be given him!"* What a wonderful promise!

Proverbs is a book of practical ethics. The purpose of the book is spelled out in its first chapter:

> *To know wisdom and instruction; to perceive the words of understanding; To receive the instruction of wisdom, justice, and judgment, and*

equity; To give subtilty to the simple, to the young man knowledge and discretion.
Proverbs 1:2-4

I have had the privilege of knowing men and women of great wisdom, and I have marveled to see how they dealt with people, how they responded to problems, how they reacted to certain situations. I have learned from such people, but nothing can replace learning from God Himself. How blessed we are to be able to sit in His presence as often as we choose and receive of His great wisdom!

We may begin these sessions with a time of worship in which we give Him the honor due His Name. We may give Him thanks for the great things He has done, and we may also bring our requests before Him. But we also need to quietly listen to Him as He speaks to us. As Jesus said:

My sheep hear my voice, and I know them, and they follow me.   John 10:27

We can tune our ears to hear God's voice. It's like using a radio. If you want to listen to British Broadcasting on a shortwave radio, you must tune to a certain wavelength. If you tune to some other frequency, you will get a different voice.

For example, before the Berlin Wall came down,

Radio Moscow aired much propaganda on short-wave radio. The setting was very close on the dial to the British Broadcasting Company. There was quite a distance, however, between the truth proclaimed by the British and the propaganda Radio Moscow was spreading.

We must be careful to hear the truth and be cautious in deciding whom we will listen to. Not all voices are good or righteous. So we must tune in to the right voices. As we delve together into the book of Proverbs, let us learn to listen to Wisdom's voice, the voice of God Himself.

Introduction

As I grew up, I had dreams of what I wanted to do, who I wanted to be. In my home I was encouraged to study hard and seek after a good education. God blessed me to be able to attend college and go on to get a professional degree in dentistry. I continued through the years to seek after knowledge, not just in medically-related subjects, but knowledge in general.

My brother told me about a series of books called *The Great Books of the Western World*. I decided to get this series for myself. It was such a complete study of the writings of the greatest thinkers of all the ages that St. John's College in Annapolis, Maryland gave a Bachelor of Arts degree for completing studies in these books. The required readings included works on the sciences, philosophy, mathematics, and literature—to just name a few of the subjects. Homer, Socrates, Plato, Chaucer, Shakespeare, Dickens and

Melville were some of the authors to be studied. As my work schedule permitted, I devoted as much time as possible to studying *The Great Books*. I found this to be a fascinating study.

There was a great sense of fulfillment as I progressed through the series. I felt that I would be able to converse intelligently on many subjects from these studies, and I felt very proud of what I was accomplishing.

My study guide occasionally recommended "supplemental readings," and the supplemental readings were from the Bible. I began to read some of the scriptural portions that were recommended. What I found was an absolute revelation. It didn't take me long to discover that the Bible contained wisdom far beyond the great minds I had been studying. Soon I was spending more time in the Bible than in *The Great Books*.

I eventually concluded that the inclusion of the Bible as "supplemental reading" in that respected course was an admission that the writings of the greatest minds of all generations could not compare with the wisdom of God Almighty, that the wisdom of the creature could never compare with the wisdom of the Creator. I had found God's truth, and it was far more invigorating and exciting than anything I had ever read before.

One of my most important biblical discoveries was

the book of Proverbs, the Book of Wisdom of the Old Testament. Although the entire Bible contains wisdom, from Genesis to Revelation, wisdom itself is the principle subject of Proverbs. Therefore, I have studied it and restudied it, taught it and retaught it, and recommended it to others many times over through the years. Proverbs is a gold mine of insight into the most important aspects of life.

And why is this important today? We are living in what has been called the information age and are bombarded on every side by the "wisdom" of our time. For every problem in life, there seems to be an innumerable host of experts ready to tell us what to do and how to live our lives to the fullest. But are they actually experts? Are they really wise? Sometimes listening to such "experts" can get us into the most terrible predicaments. At the very least it can be confusing, since these experts often cannot seem to agree on the correct solutions to our problems.

Now more than ever, God's people must turn a deaf ear to the wisdom of this world and open ourselves to the Source of all true wisdom — God Himself. The wisdom presented to us in God's Holy Word far surpasses that found in any of the "information" we might encounter today.

When I taught the book of Proverbs to our Bible School class in Virginia, my pastor said to me, "You should make these lectures into a book. It would bless a lot of people." That was several years and several books ago, but I believe it is now God's time to use the material of this book for His glory. My prayer is that you might be enriched and enlarged in your spiritual life as you read and as you make God's wisdom your own.

Dr. Jerry Kirchner
Ashland, Virginia

- 1 -

The Value of Wisdom

To know wisdom and instruction; to perceive the words of understanding; To receive the instruction of wisdom, justice, and judgment, and equity; To give subtilty to the simple, to the young man knowledge and discretion.

Proverbs 1:2-4

If we know a goal is valuable, we don't mind putting some time and effort into reaching it. Is wisdom valuable? Are understanding and instruction worthy goals? One of the clearly stated purposes of the book of Proverbs is to show us the value of wisdom and to motivate us to seek it. The word *wise* is used sixty-six times in this book; *wisdom* and *understanding* are both used fifty-four times, and *knowledge* is used forty-two times. This is a book worth reading, one that can change not only our understanding, but also our lives.

Proverbs begins with a statement of purpose. It tells us what we are to receive as we read and study its teachings. But what does it mean to give *"subtilty to the simple"*? Who are the simple? *Simple* generally refers to people of limited education. Simple people are frequently naive. Too often, when they open their mouths, others immediately become aware of their limitations. They have no subtlety.

Such people are easily deceived. But God has determined that His people will not be deceived. So when we read that part of the purpose of the book of Proverbs is *"to give subtlety to the simple,"* we can understand that God intends to place within His people a sense of knowing the genuine from the false. The wisdom of God will protect you when men lie to you, when they try to deceive you and, most of all, when they try to tell you something contrary to the Word of God. What a wonderful God we serve!

The wisdom of God is so essential for those of us who want to walk holy in this sinful world in which we live. This age demands of us great wisdom. People are facing situations today that previous generations never had to face. The Word of God will strengthen us to know how to withstand any attack of the enemy.

In these difficult times, it takes great wisdom to know just how to proceed. We need *"knowledge and discretion."* Each of us must be teachable, willing to listen, willing to allow God to lead.

Many of the voices calling out in the world today sound logical and correct. If we are not warned against wrong teachings, we may be easily taken in by them. A wise man, however, will hear what God is saying as He speaks through His Word, through His servants the prophets, and through the leadership He places in the Church.

It is not uncommon for those who are young in the Lord to walk in constant confusion. "Is this God?" they ask themselves, "Or is this me? Or is it, perhaps, the devil?" We need to know for certain whose voice we are hearing, or we may walk down wrong paths. The Bible is our *"necessary food"* and holds wisdom for each day.

Along with the wisdom that it teaches, Proverbs is also a book of warnings. Although we may consider warnings to be negative, they can save our lives and keep us on right paths.

Proverbs also teaches the idea of personal responsibility. God is looking for mature and maturing men and women who will be responsible to do His will, working to accomplish His purposes. He is looking for those whom He can trust to do certain tasks. I did not fully realize this when I was led of the Lord to enter full-time ministry. I assumed that God would entrust His work to anyone willing to do it.

I was disappointed when my dentistry practice did not sell as quickly as I had imagined it would. As time went on, I grew irritated and restless as I thought about the vast harvest fields awaiting Ginny and me. I prayed, "Lord, the harvest fields are ripe with grain and the workers are so few. Here are two that are ready to go."

But God answered, "No, you're not. You're not ready yet. You haven't fully prepared yourselves, and I won't send you until you are prepared."

Thank God that He knows what's ahead! He sees what will happen, and He won't let us go and make a mess of things.

Sometimes when we are young and have learned a little, we feel we are totally ready to face life. We imagine that we can conquer anything, do anything. Thank God that He knows better and helps us prepare for what lies ahead!

"I don't sponsor failure," God told me. "Get yourself ready. You're not going to go to other countries to make a mess of things. You're going there to represent Me."

I had much to learn before I could be sent out to minister the Gospel. I had the desire; I had the zeal; but I lacked the wisdom and that is what God had to teach me before I could be successful as a minister for Him.

Our society thrives on immediate gratification. We have fast food and drive-through banks. I had imagined that as soon as I was willing to work for God,

He would be glad to send me out to minister. I didn't realize that there was a training time involved, a time of maturing and growing in wisdom before God could entrust to me His work. We often see this impatience in the young people we talk with.

Young people often fix their attention on successful people and try to imitate them. But too often they choose the wrong people to emulate. The hardest thing for many young people who give their hearts to Jesus seems to be to separate themselves from their worldly friends, from their worldly amusements and from their worldly music. But these things will drag believers down.

Younger believers sometimes assume that by maintaining their ties to former friends and by continuing to go to the same places, they will win many other young people for Christ. But it doesn't generally happen that way. Those who continue to associate with the same people and to frequent the same places wind up being dragged back into sin, not the other way around.

Young people have great zeal, but zeal without wisdom is dangerous.

It doesn't necessarily take twenty-five years to become wise. It can take a long time, or it can happen quickly; but it must happen, or you will not prosper in your Christian walk.

How can you increase in wisdom? You need to

spend some time in fasting and prayer. You need to spend time before the Lord learning to know His voice and listening to what He will tell you specifically. You need to do whatever is necessary for you, as an individual, to rise up in the Spirit of God and take your place as a wise and mature believer. Anything that is worth having in this world costs something, and the more valuable things always cost more. Don't be afraid to pay any price to get wisdom.

If you want an old broken-down car, you can have that. But, personally, I need something that is reliable and that will get me where I need to go. So I am willing to pay a little more. What about you?

You may have to make some sacrifices in order to reach your goal. You may have to set some priorities in life and decide that you can do without some things if you are to obtain what is really important to you. That's important to obtain your goal.

If your goals include growing in wisdom and maturity in God, you can think of the book of Proverbs as an instruction manual. You can't do a job properly these days without one. Every manufacturer must provide a complete guide to the products he produces. And Proverbs is a spiritual guidebook.

I don't blame people for rejecting outdated products or ideas. We could not survive as a society by using the manufacturing methods of the last century. Technology is currently developing at such a rapid rate that machines become obsolete within a few years. But the wisdom of God's Word is just as applicable today as it ever was. Everything we need to be successful in Christian life and in ministry can be found in it. Don't try to do the work without first reading the manual. Don't try to operate the equipment without first learning more about it. The Bible is a very practical book, as fresh as today's headlines.

Wisdom for the believer is not just an option. We need the wisdom of God to know and understand what He wants us to do with our lives. We need to be able to discern His plans for us. Otherwise, we may be just putting in time rather than accomplishing to the fullest what we are capable of doing under His direction.

I learned this lesson while I was still working in my business. I was attending some meetings at Ashland Campground in Virginia, and while I was there, a lady had said to me, "Dr. Jerry, the Lord showed me that you're doing an important work." I was happy to hear that. Sometimes we're not really sure about the importance of what we are doing.

But that wasn't the end of her comment. She continued, "Yes, God showed me that what you're doing is important. But you know, unbelievers can do what you're doing." That blew all the wind out of my sails!

What she said was true. Unbelievers could have

done what I was doing at that time. Her comments made me realize I could be replaced by an unbeliever in my job so that I could be released to do a supernatural work for God. You may be the best secretary they've ever had in your company. You may be the most qualified person who has ever taken a computer training course. You may be a gifted musician. I'm sure that there are many things you can do well. But in the natural sense there may be another person who can replace you in that job so that you may be released to do a work for God. We need to seek God's wisdom for what He wants us to do with our lives.

Because of my background, God often uses Ginny and me to minister to professional people, frequently in Full Gospel Businessmen's chapters. When professionals hear that a dentist or medical doctor is going to speak, they may come to a meeting out of curiosity. That happens to us many times. When we were in Indonesia and Malaysia, many doctors came to hear us speak. In Third-World countries, professionals enjoy great prestige, to a much higher degree than here in America. They feel very important, and they let you know that they are the medical examiner for the state, or a surgeon in charge of the orthodontics or orthopedic department at a university.

Then I stand up and tell how I used to teach at the University of Maryland and belonged to the American Academy of General Dentistry. That gives us a common bond. I go on to tell them what God did in my life and how He changed me and made me a minister to go out to the world and preach the Gospel. I tell them about the lady's words to me: If you're doing a natural job, natural men can replace you. Most professional people don't seem to like to hear that very much. They're happy doing what they're doing, especially if it brings them prestige.

But God has a perfect will for every one of us. We need to have the sensitivity to hear His voice and to be guided by Him. We need the knowledge that He gives so that we can live our lives as He desires.

Proverbs can bring us *"knowledge and discretion,"* — just what we need to grow in wisdom and maturity. I find it interesting that verse 4 specifically refers to young men. Young men are not always very wise. They may do foolish things. I don't know why the Lord specifically mentions young men, but as we read the book of Proverbs we'll find there are many things that men do that will get them into a lot of trouble. We all need the wisdom of God and the knowledge of God which can only come from a direct relationship with Jesus Christ. We need to be mature, responsible people of prayer. Spend time in the book of Proverbs and you will grow in wisdom.

We need wisdom to speak intelligently with the people around us. Don't argue with people about spiritual matters. You won't win anyone that way.

Our job is to win people, not to irritate them. But do try to converse with people on subjects that interest them.

I don't know very much about politics, or government, or the financial circles of this world, but God knows all about those things, and gives the knowledge to speak about them. Just like Jesus and the woman at the well, we speak first of the natural things, and then lead into the spiritual things:

> *Jesus therefore, being wearied with His journey, sat thus on the well: and it was about the sixth hour. There cometh a woman of Samaria to draw water: Jesus saith unto her, Give me to drink. ... Then saith the woman of Samaria unto him, How is it that thou, being a Jew, askest drink of me, which am a woman of Samaria? For the Jews have no dealings with the Samaritans. Jesus answered and said unto her, If thou knewest the gift of God ...*   John 4:6-10

I had to learn that I could not win the well-educated people with my intellectual arguments and I had to learn not to begin our conversation with theological subjects. Jesus said to the woman at the well: "*Give Me to drink.*" From there, He went on to bring her into eternal life.

Samaritans and Jews were enemies who didn't

even speak to each other, but Jesus got that woman to talk with Him, and He got her to listen to what He had to say. He knows how to do that. If He had begun with the need for living water, she might not have listened to Him, but He knew how to begin. There is a proper way to do things.

God will give us wisdom in speaking with unbelievers. He will enable us to draw them to Him, to center the conversation on those things that are true and eternal. But He will teach us to do it as Jesus did.

We don't walk up to someone with our Bibles open and say, "You know, it says in John 3:3 that you need to be born again." While that may be true, it's not the way to begin a conversation with an unsaved person. Jesus led people from the natural to the supernatural, and that's what you and I must learn to do.

If we are to *"receive the instruction of wisdom,"* we must first reorient our thinking and realize what is really valuable in life. If you go to a museum, or to a jeweller's, you will see many beautiful jewels there: sapphires, emeralds, rubies, and diamonds. These are natural treasures. They satisfy for a time, but there are genuine and enduring treasures, and it is these that we must be seeking.

You and I must not be guided by what we find in our wallets. You might not have much money in this world, but wisdom is something no man can take from you. Seek those things that are eternal, that produce life, and that cannot be destroyed. Keep your eyes on the eternal things of God.

The devil knows his time is short, and so he is doing all he can to overcome believers. He would love to draw us away from our Lord, and he will use anything in his power to do so. If we don't keep our eyes on Jesus and the things of eternity, we can be turned aside by the things of this world. But we've come too far to turn aside now. We must not look back, but go forward in victory with Jesus, learning to use His wisdom.

The Lord gives *"knowledge and discretion."* He says to us, *"This is the way, walk ye in it."* We need to listen to the words of discretion the Lord gives us. He may say, "These are ungodly friends. Stay away from them." "This woman will lead you into trouble. Avoid her." That is discretion. The very next verse tells us, *"A wise man will hear..."* God has given us ears for the purpose of hearing. We're not to listen to every bit of gossip that is going around. We're not to listen to every report, because many contain discouragement and fear. But we are to listen to the voice of the Lord, and to the word of discretion that He gives each of us:

> *A wise man will hear, and will increase learning; and a man of understanding shall attain unto wise counsels.*   Proverbs 1:5

The wise not only hear, they also learn. They *"increase learning."* There are people who have been on this road a lot longer than I have, and I can sit and listen to such people and learn more in five minutes than others could teach me in two hours. We need to find teachers who will encourage us, not discourage us. We need to find teachers who are experienced in God, and in working with people. They will show you practical things. They will teach us from their experience, not merely what should work in theory. Learning from such people is an enriching experience.

> *To understand a proverb, and the interpretation;*
> *the words of the wise, and their dark sayings.*
>   Proverbs 1:6

"To understand a proverb." It really does us no good if we read a proverb and fail to understand it. The Lord desires to give us understanding in these things. They should not be mysteries to us if we are willing to search them out.

If a person is not very knowledgeable in mathematics, and they try to understand a book of advanced mathematics, it will be very confusing to them.

If they are willing to spend time in that text and analyze it and get someone qualified to teach it to them, then it may open up to them and they will understand it. The Word of God is just like that. Parts of it are understandable to a child, and other parts seem to be confusing at first. So we study those parts more, to get the meaning of them.

God wants us to be able to interpret His holy Word so that we can administer it to others. We must be able to break it down, step by step, and analyze it for ourselves when studying these early verses of Proverbs. We may begin by asking questions: What do I know about wisdom? How can I know more about wisdom? What kind of wisdom is God talking about? What will this do for me? How can I apply it?

As we continue to study together the book of Proverbs, let us seek after the wisdom that only God gives. Let us understand that wisdom is necessary if we are to come to maturity in God, to do His will and to accomplish His purposes for our lives. Let us learn the value of wisdom.

The Fear of the Lord

The fear of the LORD is the beginning of knowledge: but fools despise wisdom and instruction.

Proverbs 1:7

"The fear of the Lord" is one of the major themes of the book of Proverbs — understandably so, since it is *"the beginning of knowledge."* If we can enthrone God in the place of honor and respect that He deserves, everything else will fall into line in our lives.

When the Bible speaks of *"the fear of the Lord,"* it doesn't refer to fear as we commonly understand the word. We need not be afraid of God.

In our present society, we are seldom told that we should fear God, yet we live in an age of other fears. People everywhere are submitting themselves to counselors who hold forth the hope of helping them overcome their terrible fears. This kind of fear is not of God and is a very destructive force. It is the fear of the Lord that sets us free from all other fears.

The future economic well-being of the world and the proliferation of pollution that threatens the planet are two of the common fears of the moment. Many fear violence or the spread of AIDS. There seem to be so many reasons to live in fear. But God has said to His people, *"Fear not!"*

We don't all have the same fears. You may have some that I have never experienced, and I may have some that you have never known. Whether we face a fear of darkness, of heights, of enclosed spaces, or of conflict, they are really not so very different. Whatever fears we may face, the answer to each is the same. Our fears represent a lack of confidence in God. If we hold Him in holy reverence, nothing will cause us to waver. We will know that He is greater than all our fears.

Knowing Christ is a lasting answer to fear. When we become believers in Him, when we know that we are washed in the blood of the Lamb and that we have an eternal home in Heaven, we lose the constant sense of fear and learn to live in hope in God. We learn to trust in Him and in His lovingkindness toward us.

Understanding the sovereignty of God and submitting ourselves to His control, we receive His protection and need fear nothing that men may do to us. Because of our trust in God, we have nothing to fear when we face the daily situations of life. We know that He is greater than all our fears.

> *There is no fear in love; but perfect love casteth out fear: because fear hath torment. He that feareth is not made perfect in love.* 1 John 4:18

As we trust in God and in His love for us, fearing and reverencing Him alone, we will come to know the truth of this verse. As we come to know His love, we are set free from fear.

The reason *"the fear of the Lord is the beginning of knowledge"* is that our God is the only One who holds the power of life and death. Satan can torment us, as we all know, but it is only our sovereign God who has power over the ultimate destination of our souls. Jesus said:

> *And fear not them which kill the body, but are not able to kill the soul: but rather fear him which is able to destroy both soul and body in hell.* Matthew 10:28

The only One we ought to fear is the One who can cast our souls into Hell. We're not to fear those who can only kill us. Neither the devil nor man can cast us into Hell. Let us develop a holy and reverential fear of God so that other things cannot control us. Then nothing else can concern us, overcome us, or cause us discouragement, or depression ... and we can live in the positive promises of God.

When you learn to live in the positive promises of God, nothing can harm you. When you recognize who God is, you soon recognize who you are in Him. That is when you lose all fear. As you begin to see who God is, you recognize your great potential in Him and you are soon changed into something far greater than you had imagined you could be.

Fear of failure is one of the most powerful and debilitating forces at work in the world today. In God, however, we cannot fail, for He cannot fail. We may have some temporary defeats in our lives; but if we understand the greatness of God and our ultimate victory in Him, we can learn from our mistakes, get up, and go forth to defeat the giants of this world.

The Apostle Paul wrote that he was *"born out of due time"* (1 Corinthians 15:8). By that he meant that he had never had the opportunity to walk with Jesus as the other apostles had. But Paul went on to become the greatest of all apostles. Why? Because he was determined to catch up, to mature in God. Determine to make yourself available to God and you can turn your limitations into strengths for the glory of God. Stop letting fear of failure hold you back.

Fools despise wisdom and instruction.
                                              Proverbs 1:7

If it is foolish to despise God's wisdom. Therefore we must adopt the opposite attitude. We must seek it, long for it, welcome it and rejoice in it. We are not to be as a fool, who doesn't listen because he thinks he already knows the truth. A fool will not heed instruction because he thinks he knows better than everyone else around him.

When my class graduated from dental school, some of my classmates had the idea that they knew everything they would ever need to know about dentistry. That was a foolish attitude that I am sure some of them soon regretted. We were only just beginning to learn.

As medical science advances, our present knowledge will be totally obsolete within seven to ten years. By that time, text books will have been revised many times. Anyone who doesn't keep learning will simply be out of touch. When we graduate from a given course of study, we like to think that we know it all, when, in reality, we have only experienced a commencement. We are only beginning to know all that we will need to know in the future to successfully carry out our chosen profession.

To keep up with new advances in dentistry, I had to attend postgraduate courses and state and national conventions. I had to become familiar with current research in the professional journals so that I knew how to apply new developments, for my own benefit and that of my patients.

It is this way in the Church as well. I have seen the most spiritual people I know take notes as others taught. You don't know it all, and I *don't* know it all. In fact, the more I learn, the more I realize how much I don't know. We will never stop learning in this life. And if we are to grow in wisdom, the first thing we need to learn is the fear of the Lord.

We have no reason to "fear" God in the common sense of the word. While He does have a right hand of judgment, He also has a left hand of mercy. He loves every one of His children and wants to do for us what we cannot do for ourselves. His judgment was not meant for you, as a child of God. Rather, His mercy is for you. His compassion is for you. His joy is for you.

I'm not a very big man, but I boldly walk down the streets of the world's cities and fear no danger for I know that God is with me. How wonderful! My wife and I felt perfect peace in the streets of Northern Ireland at the height of the conflict. We didn't know where a terrorist's bomb might be planted, but we did know we were safe in Jesus. We felt perfect peace in the streets of the former Soviet Union when terror reigned all around us. I felt perfect peace in the Buddhist Temples of Tibet. God's peace can reign in our lives regardless of outward circumstances.

The Scriptures promise:

> *The angel of the Lord encampeth round about
> them that fear him, and delivereth them.*
>
> Psalm 34:7

When we believe and trust in God, we can know
His peace.

David declared:

> *Yea, though I walk through the valley of the
> shadow of death, I will fear no evil: for Thou art
> with me; thy rod and thy staff they comfort me.*
>
> Psalm 23:4

Whether you live in a quiet neighborhood or next
door to a crack house, whether you live in a land of
peace and prosperity or in a war-torn country, God
can make the place where you dwell a haven of rest
and security, a place of safety.

Do you live in a place of darkness? Perhaps God
has strategically placed you there as a light in the
midst of that darkness. Shine for Him! He can bring
you peace in the midst of the most violent storm.

When God called my wife and I to work for Him,
we said, "We'll go anywhere, Lord," and we meant
it. Through our travels in some sixty countries, God
has been faithful to keep us, but we have had to be
faithful in refusing to live in fear. As we trusted in
God, He has kept us in peace.

One time, while we were in India, Ginny contracted malaria. We were told, "Once you have malaria, you can expect a recurrence of it every six months." I believed what we were told.

From India we traveled to Indonesia. As we traveled, I was counting the days, expecting Ginny to get sick again. Sure enough, six months after the first occurrence, she again became ill. I was forced to go out to the villages without her, leaving her suffering in her bed with malaria. I so missed her and her help in ministering to the many spiritually hungry and needy people that I decided that it was ridiculous to limit ourselves in this way. We simply couldn't go on living our life like that, expecting her to be sick every six months. So we refused to live under that fear. Once we took this stand and refused to live in constant fear, the malaria never recurred again.

Several times during our years of traveling I became so ill that I thought I might die. But I would say to myself, "Why did I have to come all the way over here to die? God didn't send me here to die. He sent me here to bring life." And I quickly recovered — God's wisdom brings us such miracles, delivering us from all fear.

Proverbs is a book of positive Christian thinking. You may have read other books about positive thinking, but Proverbs teaches positive Christian thinking in a godly way. As you grow in righteousness, you'll realize that God has an answer to all things. The answer is in the Word of God and in living a holy life. The answer lies in turning away from the world and in being overcomers – being overcomers by facing things with God's help rather than alone. We must find our strength in God. We must know who we are in Him and fear Him only.

We need not fear failure, because there are no failures and no successes in God's economy. It is all part of God's plan. People become elated and excited about victories in their lives, and discouraged and depressed about the things that they call "failures." But apart from the failures of sin, everything that happens to us is part of God's plan. Not all of the things that we term "failures" are ordered by the Lord, but He allows them, and they all work out for our good, and often for the good of others. How can we be anything but joyful?

This is why Proverbs is such an important book: It teaches us right thinking and it gives us the desire to become mature individuals in God. The beginning of the knowledge that we each need to minister in Jesus' Name is found in *"the fear of the Lord."*

As we mature in God, we increase in our love for Him. When we love Him, when we really know Him, hearing His voice and seeing His face, then the things of this world no longer matter. The sacrifices we make no longer matter.

My wife and I, as we have traveled around the

nations of the world, have met many people whose lives are sacrificial, and even though God sends us out to bless others, many times we gain a greater blessing when we see the price others have paid.

On one of our trips to China, to minister and to deliver Bibles to the believers there, we told the people how we in America had been praying for them and how blessed and grateful we were that God has given them favor with their government. They were free to publish the Bible in three Chinese cities.

Then we listened as they told us about what their lives had been like. Some had just come from prison — after eleven years or more. But they hadn't hardened their hearts. They were not angry about it. They were not blaming the government. "There was much turmoil at that time, and the government leaders really thought they were doing what was best for the people," they explained. It was amazing to hear them speak in this way! We could see the sweetness and the anointing on their lives. No wonder God is blessing their nation with great revival!

The search for wisdom and the fear of God are strongly linked in scripture:

> *My son, if thine heart be wise, my heart shall rejoice, even mine.*   Proverbs 23:15

> *Let not thine heart envy sinners: but be thou in*
> *the fear of the LORD all the day long.*
>   Proverbs 23:17

These themes are seen throughout the book of Proverbs. Why? Because the fear of the Lord is *"the beginning of wisdom."* All of God's blessings and anointings flow from this root. If we will put Him first, He will lead us into a higher understanding of His way and His will for our lives. And once we have laid hold of God's wisdom and truth, we must never lay it aside:

> *Buy the truth, and sell it not: also wisdom, and*
> *instruction, and understanding.*
>   Proverbs 23:23

Wisdom wants to walk in the truth and speak the truth. Wisdom wants to do that which pleases God, for as we seek to please our Lord, we are positioned to receive His great provision.

We have experienced this rich provision of the Lord as we have traveled throughout the world, and we have seen it at work in the lives of others as well. On one of our early trips to China, we were surprised and blessed to see a brother, a bishop from Norway, speaking in a church. We had been told that foreigners couldn't minister there at all; but there he was, preaching to the people via an interpreter. That openness is part of God's provision for the Chinese believers.

As we traveled in China we met young people at six seminaries or training centers. These young believers are serious about serving God. They make great sacrifices to attend these training centers for about two years. Their churches support them as they study, but they live in difficult circumstances. There is no heat in the buildings, and the food supply is very meager. These students don't have much, but they feel very privileged to be able to study the Bible. They are paying the price to *"buy the truth."*

Proverbs promises that our search for wisdom will cause us to *"understand the fear of the Lord"*:

> *If thou seekest her as silver, and searchest for her as for hid treasures; Then shalt thou understand the fear of the LORD, and find the knowledge of God.*   Proverbs 2:4-5

When we seek after the things of God, we are not to be halfhearted. We are to look as though for the most precious treasures; for that is exactly what we are seeking. When we find the fear of the Lord, we have found also the knowledge of God. All the things of God fit together into a beautiful pattern. There are no small and unimportant things in God.

His Word is treasure unto us, and it reveals His patterns and wisdom to us. As we are diligent to seek it, and as we *"buy"* it and *"sell not,"* God will give us His wisdom.

Yes, the wisdom the Lord imparts is more precious than silver, more precious than hidden treasures.

> *For the LORD giveth wisdom: out of his mouth cometh knowledge and understanding. He layeth up sound wisdom for the righteous: he is a buckler to them that walk uprightly.*
>
> Proverbs 2:6-7

God *"lays up sound wisdom for the righteous."* Let's enter into the righteousness of God so we can enter into that *"sound wisdom." "He is a Buckler,"* One who shields and protects. He is the strength of those who walk uprightly. We don't have to live in fear; we can live instead in trust in our God.

My wife and I do not have to fear, no matter where the Lord sends us, because we know God's strength is there. His provision is there. We have gone into places and situations that men have looked at as very dangerous. But we have been able to trust in the goodness of our God in the midst of these situations. And He has been faithful. People have told us that they have seen strong angels standing beside my wife and me as we go. We don't have to be fearful. And neither do you.

*Then shalt thou understand righteousness, and
judgment, and equity; yea, every good path.
When wisdom entereth into thine heart, and
knowledge is pleasant unto thy soul; Discretion
shall preserve thee, understanding shall keep
thee.*   Proverbs 2:9-11

When wisdom *"enters into your heart"* and *"knowledge is pleasant unto your soul,"* then you shall be kept
in understanding. You will begin to comprehend
righteousness and judgment and equality and every
good path. Your eyes will begin to be opened, the
scales will be removed, and you'll say, "God really
loves me."

Sometimes it's hard to seè God's love in a given
situation. When I still worked as a dentist, the Lord
used to wake me up at three in the morning. I wasn't
happy about it. So I complained to Him.

The Lord asked, "Jerry, why do you think I'm wak-
ing you up at three o'clock in the morning?"

I said, "I guess it's part of my training, Lord. You
must be trying to burn out some of these impurities
in me."

He said, "No, Jerry. I love you so much."

I said, "How can You call that love? I have to be
rested, Lord! I need to have a steady hand when I go
to do surgery in the morning!"

The Lord gently reminded me, "Jerry, your former
dental assistant is living in Israel, working with the

ministry team there. Do you know what time it is there when it's 3:00 a.m. here?"

I answered Him, "It's 9:00 in the morning."

He continued, "Do you know what the team in Israel is doing at 9:00 a.m.?"

I did know. They were standing in a circle holding hands and praying for the nations of the world. I had often asked the Lord if I could go and be with them during this time of prayer. The Lord reminded me of this now. He said, "You don't have the opportunity to go. But if you wake up at 3:00 AM you can be with them in the Spirit."

I was so ashamed that I had fussed with the Lord who only wanted to bless me.

> *The fear of the LORD is a fountain of life, to depart from the snares of death.* Proverbs 14:27

The fear in which the world lives is distinctive but *"the fear of the Lord"* is just the opposite. It is *"a fountain of life."* Hear God's "fear not," no matter what you face: war, strife, or any other danger. Throughout the world, there are terrifying situations that people must live through. Refuse to live in fear, but in *"the fear of the Lord."* As you look to Him, your attitude of reverence and respect for the Lord will become *"a fountain of life"* to your soul. *"Fear not"* what man can do to you. *"Fear not"* what the enemy

can do. Fear not any trouble within the land. God has
the power to keep you. God is able to preserve His
people and bring us through:

> *In the fear of the* LORD *is strong confidence: and*
> *His children shall have a place of refuge.*
>
> Proverbs 14:26

There will always be *"a place of refuge"* for God's
people, a place of safety. In the Old Testament we
read of the cities of refuge that were established by
God for His people. If a man accidentally killed another, he could run to one of those cities, there to
dwell in safety. That's how it is in our lives as well.
There is *"a place of refuge"* that God has prepared for
us and as we live in the fear of the Lord, we have the
confidence of dwelling in that place.

> *The fear of the* LORD *tendeth to life: and he that*
> *hath it shall abide satisfied; he shall not be vis-*
> *ited with evil.*   Proverbs 19:23

If you want to live a satisfied life, this is the secret.
Learn to hear the voice of God, to tap into the resources of God, and to follow His leading. When you
do this, you have a great promise. You will *"abide*
satisfied," and you shall not *"be visited with evil."*

Walking in the fear of the Lord closes the door to
evil in our lives.

Now is the time to seek out the wisdom of the Lord. Now is the time to begin to mature spiritually. Now is the time to seek after God. Now is the time to walk in *"the fear of the Lord."*

- 3 -

The Need to be Teachable

My son, hear the instruction of thy father, and forsake not the law of thy mother: For they shall be an ornament of grace unto thy head, and chains about thy neck.   Proverbs 1:8-9

These verses introduce another important aspect of the teaching of Proverbs, a theme that recurs frequently throughout the book: Listening to and heeding instruction. We all need to have teachable spirits, whether we're children or adults, although, in this particular passage, a father is speaking to his son, instructing him in wisdom and righteousness.

Parents are normally wiser than children, because they have learned many hard lessons in life. But sadly, when parents try to pass along their acquired wisdom to their children, it is often rejected. When we try to tell our children things we know will bless them and keep them from harm and danger, and they don't seem to want to take our advice, it can be disheartening. Solomon wrote:

> *My son, keep thy father's commandment, and forsake not the law of thy mother: Bind them continually upon thine heart, and tie them about thy neck.* Proverbs 6:20-21

The lessons that our parents have taught us, and those that we teach our children, are invaluable. They are the lessons of experience, to keep the hearer from trouble.

My wife and I raised five children, and we did our best to warn them of the pitfalls of life. We tried to show them how to avoid the things that had brought us trouble. Our children then didn't have to go through all the things we have gone through. Sometimes our children listened and they were blessed, but sometimes they wouldn't listen, and they had to pay the consequences. Later they were sorry and said, as many of us do, "Oh, I wish I would have listened!"

We must have ears to hear to what God is saying. He has a message for the Church day by day. I believe that just as we can read the headlines of the morning newspaper, so God can give us His message for each day, for ourselves and for those whose lives we touch. But ears must be open to hear what God is saying.

Because they are living in a different era, our children imagine that the things we try to tell them somehow don't apply to them. "That was for another time," they insist. "This is a new generation. I respect what you are saying, but it is not for me." This is the folly that has always overtaken the youth of our world. They have not yet lived long enough to appreciate the lessons older people have learned.

Some of us would have been grateful if someone had taken enough interest in us to teach us the things of God when we were younger. Now we must realize that attentiveness to wise people can save us a world of sorrow. A few moments of openness can help to prevent the tragedies of life from overtaking us. Attentiveness to truth can make all the difference in the world.

If we are willing to listen to the advice of others, we can learn in a short time what others took a lifetime to experience. Don't insist on learning everything the hard way.

We should give special attention to those we know who have been pioneers of faith. They have fought hard and paid a great price for what they have accomplished. Such people of faith have a lot to share with us — if we are willing to listen. The fact that it took them many years to come to their present knowledge should make us realize that we cannot learn it all overnight. Don't be foolish. Have a teachable spirit.

We should not take lightly the counsel of those whom God has set over us in the Church. We should submit ourselves, our activities, and our spiritual well-being to them for guidance.

If your spiritual father doesn't approve of what you are doing, there is probably a very good reason for it. He is not intent on robbing you of your fun in life. He is not intent on depriving you of opportunity in life. What he is telling you is for your own good.

This is a key element in the development of your spiritual life and ministry. Learn it well. You don't have to repeat all the same mistakes others have made — if you will listen to others carefully when they try to warn you of the pitfalls that caught them unprepared. You can learn from them and avoid the pain they suffered.

It hurts a parent's heart to see a child suffer, but there is only so much the parent can do to prevent it. Children have their own minds and make their own decisions. So it is up to each of us to make the right decisions. If we learn to heed our elders, we can avoid much pain. If not, sometimes we may reap the consequences of our mistakes for years to come.

Having a teachable spirit is not only for children. We cannot say, "Well, I'm mature now. I'm older and these things don't apply to me." The Word of God does not say that when you get to be nineteen or twenty-one, you are on your own. We are to learn from those who have gone before us at whatever age we find ourselves. If we are not willing to learn from others' experiences, we will bring ourselves a lot of trouble.

As my wife and I have ministered in prisons, inmates have told us that they thank God they're in prison. That seems like a surprising statement. Who would want to end up in prison? It's not exactly the kind of place that you'd sign up for if you had a choice. But these prisoners thank God for it. You see, when they were out on the streets they were running as hard as they could from God. He had to bring them to a place where they could no longer run. Then someone was able to come and preach the Word to them. As a consequence, they found a new way of living; and a new reason to live.

That's why they're thanking God, not because they're in prison or because they are separated from their families, and not for the loss of their freedom. They are thanking God that they found something better than running around in this world trying to get rich and causing trouble. How much easier, how much less painful it would have been for these people to have allowed themselves to learn from others instead of having to be brought to such a low state!

*Bow down thine ear, and hear the words of the
wise, and apply thine heart unto my knowledge.*
                                        Proverbs 22:17

Ours has been called "the information age." Everyone seems to be searching for more and more
knowledge, but so much of it is carnal. It is time to
"bow [our] ear and hear the words of the wise."

Be teachable. Receive wisdom, not only from the
Lord, but also from His people, from those whom He
has set into our lives to help and guide us.

It takes humility to receive from others, but those
who are more mature in the Lord are set into our
lives for a purpose. We are to allow the Lord to share
His wisdom with us through them. No matter how
long we've been in the ministry, no matter how
much we may think we know, we need to be teachable.

It is not enough even to *"bow [our] ears and hear."*
We need to receive that which is spoken, and take it
as God's wisdom into the depths of our being:

*My son, if thou wilt receive my words, and hide
my commandments with thee; So that thou in-
cline thine ear unto wisdom, and apply thine
heart to understanding; Yea, if thou criest after
knowledge, and liftest up thy voice for understanding ... Then shalt thou understand the fear
of the* LORD.   Proverbs 2:1-3, 5

We cannot simply seek after knowledge for the sake of knowledge or wisdom for the sake of wisdom. Our search has a goal: to *"understand the fear of the Lord."* Earthly wisdom and earthly knowledge does not recognize the fear of the Lord. We seek a higher wisdom, godly wisdom.

Each of us may have a different level of education, but that really doesn't matter. We are all equal in the sight of God because it's not our wisdom that is important, *it's His wisdom.* I graduated from college and from dental school, and I also taught at dental school. My wife graduated from her college with honors. But none of these things qualify us to do what we're doing. Our ability is in God. It is the wisdom and knowledge that He imparts that qualifies us to minister in His Name.

If you want wisdom and understanding, then you must have your ears open to hear what God is saying through others. He wants to speak to us personally and instruct us in what to do, what to say, what portion of Scripture to read for the day, where to focus our attention. I believe we should have a balance in the reading of the Bible, not specializing in a small portion alone. And each of us must be a student of the Word. If we do not understand something we read there, we can ask God to show us what it means. But we must also listen as we are being taught by others. Listen carefully when a prophetic word goes forth. Don't let it fall to the ground. Take it and apply it to your heart.

Many years ago God sent me to a Charismatic Bible school for a short time. I was invited to speak to the students, who were training to be used in full-time service to the Lord. I thought I was going there to teach them for many days, but God had a different plan.

When I arrived on a Monday, the young man who met me at the airport said, "We have you scheduled to speak to the students on Friday morning." I was quite surprised. I thought they surely would give me more time than that. What would I be doing the rest of the week?

I heard God say, "Oh, there's a job you're going to do here. In fact, there are several jobs. And you *are* going to speak on Friday morning, but you are also going to listen to others."

Sometimes we need to listen instead of speaking so much. I learned a bit about that while I was in that place.

As I walked the campus that week, I found that there were married couples who needed counseling and encouragement in their daily relationships with God and each other. I found that the Catholic, Episcopal, and Methodist churches were working together with the school itself. I hadn't seen denominational groups working together like that before, so it was enlightening to me. I sat in the classes with the students, and I listened to the teachers. I studied the attitudes of the students. You can learn a lot by simply looking, listening, and praying that God will direct you into the things He wants you to know.

I learned quite a bit about intercession through the intercessory groups which met at lunch time each day. Students from various geographical locations, sometimes from three or four countries, met together to pray for their particular part of the world.

I was so blessed to learn much in that place. And when it came time to speak on Friday, I was pleased to find that the students were also teachable. When I stood before the students to speak, I said, "God has shown me many things since I've been here. He shows me that you have faith. Some of you came here quite young in the Lord, knowing little of God or of the provision of God, but you had the faith to believe that God could save your soul and He could send you to Bible school and teach you. You had the faith that He would provide for you.

"You have hope. You had the hope that if you did your work, paid attention to the teachers, and disciplined yourself, if you prayed and read the Word of God, some day you would graduate and become a Bible teacher, or an evangelist, or a missionary to the world. You had the hope that all your study and work would not be in vain, but that you would be prepared to do the work of the Lord. You have faith and you have hope, but there are many students here who lack love."

In that moment, I wondered where the Holy Spirit was leading me with this. I didn't even know these people! How would they respond? But I felt God leading me so I continued. The students there went to school in the morning and had jobs in the afternoon to support themselves and their families and to pay for their education. They were so involved with their jobs and their families and with getting out of the classes what they could that many didn't have time to notice the person next to them. God told me to tell them, "If you can't love the person next to you, you're never going to be a success on the mission field. These are familiar surroundings. You know the culture; you're familiar with the food. Everything is comfortable and familiar. But when you go to a foreign country, everything is totally unfamiliar to you. You must learn to love one another. If you cannot love one another here, you will never be able to do it there."

I left the platform to find that the students were weeping. Many of them came to me and said, "Thank God, He sent you here to tell us such a thing. Nobody ever told us anything like that before, but it's true."

We had a time of weeping and repenting that

morning. Those students had teachable spirits. They wanted what God had for them. And even when it required repentance and a changing of their own ways, they had the wisdom to follow.

God showed us this when we went to Indonesia. We had thought all the details were settled and ready for us to go and minister there, but the government had changed the visa requirements. The interpreter came to me and said, "Dr. Jerry, it's not going to work out very well. You will not be able to go out of the main city of Djakarta to preach in Central or East Java or in other islands. You need a special visa for that. We couldn't get you one because we didn't know about it in time. You have to get it in advance. You need the approval of the government and approved invitations from three churches."

We had planned to be in Indonesia for six weeks. Now we were being told that nothing would get done because we couldn't get out of the capital city. What should we do? Was this to be a wasted trip? We had hoped to travel and minister from village to village.

And when we asked the Lord about this unexpected change of plans, He said, "There are seven million people in this city. There are three to five thousand islands in Indonesia. You can't get to them all anyway. But even if you can't get to them, I can send them to you." What a good God we serve!

Our first thought had been, "What a disaster!" But it was all part of God's plan to do great things for us. This is how He works. He wants to do great things for us, but we must have our ears open and be teachable.

We could not have gone to all of those islands, no matter how much time we had. So what did God do? He sent the ministers from many of those islands so we could hold a ministers' conference. This brought a multiplication of the ministry. As they were taught and ministered to, they could teach and minister to others. Thank God that we were teachable and open to God's plans.

Proverbs speaks of those who were not teachable as "the foolish." The foolish, according to the Word, are those who do not seek after the ways of God. They are those who, when faced with a difficult situation, plunge ahead to do whatever they think right, without seeking wise counsel from God or man:

> *The way of a fool is right in his own eyes: but he that hearkeneth unto counsel is wise.*
>
> Proverbs 12:15

It is very sad when people won't listen to wise counsel. We have to wonder what's wrong with them and why they refuse to be teachable. They are only hurting themselves. This attitude doesn't seem to have any relationship to age, status, experience, or geography. There are unteachable people in every nation and in every strata of life.

In the natural, if a man refuses to be taught, he cannot take on a new work. He may lose his job and be replaced by another. Those who refuse to learn the things of the Spirit will also be passed by others moving up the ladder of God's blessing. The unteachable miss out on knowing all that God has for them, and on ministering to the full extent of God's intent. We must be soft before the Lord, ready to listen and ready to heed what He says to us.

When we try to do things in our own ability, we will soon learn the truth of the statement:

> *There is a way which seemeth right unto a man, but the end thereof are the ways of death.*
> Proverbs 14:12

It may be the *"death"* of a plan or of a vision of what we thought God was going to do. It may be the *"death"* of a relationship. It may even be a physical or a spiritual death. The result of doing things our own way and trusting our own wisdom is always disaster. Don't be as *"the foolish"* who trust to their own wisdom.

> *A reproof entereth more into a wise man than an hundred stripes into a fool.*   Proverbs 17:10

How do *you* respond to correction? If you are wise, you will love those who reprove you, and will receive and respond to their words. Allow yourself to grow in receiving correction, and in allowing the Lord to use others to speak into your life. Some people can appear to be very "spiritual" when they respond to a correction they hear the Lord bringing to them; but woe to the individual who would speak to that person with the very same correction! Let's allow every reproof to enter into our hearts and spirits.

Let a bear robbed of her whelps meet a man, rather than a fool in his folly.   Proverbs 17:12

Think about that! The Lord is saying that it would be better to meet a mother bear robbed of her cubs than to meet up with a fool in his folly. What is such a bear like? Very dangerous! Mama bears become life-threatening if their cubs are endangered. But the Lord says that a fool is even more dangerous. It is foolish to stay around such people. Get as far away from them as you possibly can.

Seest thou a man wise in his own conceit? there is more hope of a fool than of him.
Proverbs 26:12

None of us like to see conceit in others. So why should we be conceited ourselves? Listen to yourself as you grow in wisdom, and don't let your own words or attitudes set you back.

It is God's knowledge that we need, and we gain that knowledge by being teachable and sitting at the feet of those who have walked with Jesus for many years. We can also learn by reading good books by men and women who have walked with God for many years. As we do these things, we will learn the ways and the wisdom of God.

4

Learning to Trust in God

Trust in the Lord with all thine heart; and lean not unto thine own understanding. In all thy ways acknowledge Him, and He shall direct thy paths.   Proverbs 3:5-6

No matter how much training you have, how much education, how much ability or talent, no matter how brilliant you are, never place your trust in your own understanding. Don't trust in your own ability. Why? Because our human understanding is so limited. As children of the Lord, we can place our trust in Him. We can receive His wisdom, which is far higher than our own. As it is written in the book of Isaiah the prophet:

For My thoughts are not your thoughts, neither are your ways my ways, saith the Lord. For as

*the heavens are higher than the earth, so are my
ways higher than your ways, and my thoughts
than your thoughts.*   Isaiah 55:8-9

His ways far surpass ours. We come to know His
ways and His thoughts by placing our trust in Him,
allowing ourselves to *"put on the mind of Christ."* As
we are diligent in this, we can learn to walk in God's
wisdom, knowing that He will *"direct our paths."*

Sometimes our paths are not smooth. They seem to
be filled with opposition. You may go somewhere
expecting the door to open wide, expecting to hear
someone say, "Oh, thank God you're here." But what
if someone slams the door shut, saying, "Oh, no!
What are you doing here?" Does that mean it was not
God's intended path for you? Not necessarily.

Sometimes when we are on the Lord's path, there
will be opposition. Sometimes the enemy tries to re-
direct our paths. We must learn to say, "Lord, where
should I be now? What should I be going?"

Never be directed by circumstances: "Well, this is
hard. I guess it's not God's direction for me right
now." Perhaps it is hard because the devil sees just
how much it is God's will for you at that moment.

Trust in God to direct your paths. And when He
does, trust in Him to help you to walk on those
paths, regardless of circumstances. If God sends you
to someone with a message, then give it. Don't be

overly concerned with the attitudes of others, or with how your words will be received. Rather, place your trust in the Lord, and be faithful to do what He has asked you to do.

"In all your ways acknowledge Him." That "all" is an important little word. We cannot seek the Lord when it is convenient, or when we've nothing more important to do with our time. We should not seek Him only concerning the "important" things. We are to seek His direction in *"all"* our ways.

Many people pray to the Lord only when faced with a major decision or crisis. But we are to acknowledge Him *"in all [our] ways."* Just as a ship or a plane that is off course by only a very few degrees will eventually miss its mark entirely, so many badly made decisions — those made in our own understanding, without first seeking the will of the Lord — will eventually cause us to veer off our course.

We all tend to make mistakes. Then we think, "Oh, if only I hadn't said that." "If only I hadn't done that." "If only ..." "If..." "If..." "If..." But it's finished, and we cannot go back and change things. We have all failed at one time or another, but God allows these things to happen to help us so that we can learn to depend on and trust in Him alone.

"Trust in the Lord with all your heart." How are you doing in that area? Are you trusting in your job, hoping for that promotion, that raise? Are you trusting in

man, waiting for that letter, that phone call, that will open doors for you? Are you trusting in God or in man? Sometimes we think we're trusting in God, but then we proceed to tell Him how to meet our needs. Rest assured that He knows what is best, and that He loves us and will do what needs to be done.

Do you know, really know, that God is a good God, that He is One we can unreservedly trust with all our hearts? You and I are to stand and proclaim the goodness of God, declaring what He has done in our lives. Others need to know that Jesus is the God who heals us and delivers us. They need to hear that Christ can save marriages and families. As we acknowledge Him *"in all [our] ways,"* our lives will become testimonies to Him. Our words will back up what others have already seen happening in our lives.

As we *"trust in the Lord,"* not only will our testimony bless others, but we ourselves will be blessed. The promise is:

> *He that putteth his trust in the LORD shall be made fat.*   Proverbs 28:25

What does this mean? Well, obviously it's not speaking of weight problems. As we place our trust in God, we are made prosperous, both naturally and spiritually. We will be growing in Him, and in our faith toward God. As we exercise our trust, it becomes stronger, and we enter into the process of maturing in God.

There are differing levels of faith, and maturing is the process of moving from level to level. Every step up is a positive step. Many books have been written concerning positive thinking, but this is not what I mean. Simply thinking positively within ourselves, in our own strength, is not enough. We are not strong in ourselves, but in Christ.

The Apostle Paul recognized this fact. We find one hundred and thirty-five places throughout the New Testament epistles where Paul wrote, *"In Christ, I can do all things."* He could say, "I may be in a shipwreck, but I'll come back with a victory." "I may be in prison, but I'll write my greatest sermon here." We can overcome the obstacles the enemy sets in our way as we learn to trust in our God.

Some people have difficult problems to overcome, but they do overcome them through their trust in God. For instance, some of the most spiritual people we have met are behind prison walls. These believers have every opportunity to choose to do evil and to learn more of the ungodly ways that abound in such places, but they have fixed their eyes on Jesus. They know that they have found the truth and the right way of life. They are determined that those prison walls will not hinder them from walking in God.

Do you have that kind of determination? Have you settled it within yourself that nothing will cause you to fall or to fail God? God gives us every opportunity to succeed. He wants us to have a good testimony. He wants us to *be* a testimony!

As we learn to trust in the Lord alone, He brings us many good things:

> *My son, forget not my law; but let thine heart keep my commandments: For length of days, and long life, and peace, shall they add to thee. Let not mercy and truth forsake thee: bind them about thy neck; write them upon the table of thine heart: So shalt thou find favour and good understanding in the sight of God and man.*
>
> Proverbs 3:1-4

"So shall you find favor and good understanding in the sight of God and man." Consider that. Isn't that what we desire to find? FAVOR. We pray about it all the time. As we pray for missionaries, we say, "Lord, give them favor with the government. Give them favor with the people. Give them favor with the ministers who decide which ones may come in to minister at which church. Give them favor, Lord."

We pray for favor for our children, or as we go to minister or share a word with someone. And God says, "I'm going to give you favor and good understanding." Isn't that good news for those who keep the commandments of God?

"Trust in the Lord." I think this is probably one of the most important Scriptures in the Bible. Learn its foundational truth. Walk in it. The Lord will bless you, and others through you, as you learn to more deeply trust.

Part of the favor that we receive from the Lord is in prosperity. If the devil has robbed you, he must restore what he has taken sevenfold, because we're good stewards of what God puts in our hands. What we receive, we're going to use for the work of God.

Once a brother prayed for the people in a meeting, that God would bring in any money owed them. I was there, and as he prayed, I thought of all the money people owed me. I was thinking, "It won't happen for me. I'll never see that money."

But shortly afterward, someone in my family wrote to me and said, "I was reminded that I sold a piece of furniture of yours while you were overseas, and I owe you some money. Here it is." I hadn't even known anything about that money. I believe that if the brother had not prayed that way, the check would not have been sent. God knows what we don't know. He knew that people owed me money, even though I didn't know it.

God knows your needs. He knows how to meet and supply for every one of them. Aren't you glad you serve the living God?

A great part of our ability to trust Him is in getting answers to our prayers. Proverbs declares:

> *The Lord is far from the wicked: but he heareth the prayer of the righteous.*   Proverbs 15:29

I would never want to be in a position where I prayed and could not hear from God. Can you imagine such a thing? You pray, yet God does not answer. He doesn't hear the prayer of the wicked. And what about the righteous? Why wouldn't He answer our prayers? Sometimes He doesn't answer our prayers because the answer is so obvious. Sometimes it seems He doesn't answer because we're afraid of the answer. We pray, but then we do not listen carefully to His response.

Several years ago, the Lord showed Ginny and me that we would be going overseas. We had it in our heart to go to Australia or perhaps South Africa. And so we prayed, "Lord, we desire to know where it is we are to go. Lord, are we to go to Australia or South Africa?" God didn't answer. I prayed again, but God still didn't answer. When I prayed a third time, God said, "Am I only the God of Australia and South Africa?"

We sometimes limit God! We think, "It's either this or it's that." And He has to say, "No, it's neither this nor that." We must do things His way, for there is no other way.

Thank God for the ability He gives us to hear His voice. He loves us so much. When He speaks to us, we need to be quiet before Him and listen.

Listening to the Lord is our place of confidence. As we lean on His word and trust in what He speaks to us from the written Word, we come into a place of safety:

> *The fear of man bringeth a snare: but whoso putteth his trust in the LORD shall be safe.*
>
> Proverbs 29:25

People need a sense of security. They need a place to run to where they can feel, and be, safe. During the era of the Cold War, we lived in fear that someone would push the button to begin a nuclear war that would annihilate the human race. Now that the Cold War has ended, we live in fear that the thousands of nuclear weapons developed during that period will find their way into the hands of terrorist groups. So, although the world is safer in one way, it is much more dangerous in another sense.

Reading the headlines of our newspapers often brings fear to people's hearts. There seems to be a legitimate reason to fear, for terrible things are happening. Murder rates continue to rise. Drug abuse seems to be totally out of control. Teenage crime continues to thrive. Guns are too readily available to criminal elements. Therefore, sales of security systems and dead bolt locks continue to soar. Now many are using two locks on every door (and some have more). Then they add an electronic security system and a good guard dog. They may build tall walls around the house, with alarms on top of that.

Where does it all stop? It seems that some can do almost anything and still not have a sense of security. This world is full of fear.

Even if we do not fear man, there are other fears to be faced. What of the diseases that we now face — AIDS and the Ebola virus for example? And what of the renewed outbreaks of diseases such as tuberculosis and cholera, which once seemed to be eradicated from our world?

When we look at all the reasons to fear, we begin to understand the need to look to Him who blesses us with safety. Our place of security lies in trusting in the Name of the Lord, the One who saves, delivers, and protects.

Isn't it good to know that the Name of the Lord is still a strong tower for the righteous?

> *The name of the LORD is a strong tower: the righteous runneth into it, and is safe.*
>
>   Proverbs 18:10

Our pastor who has gone on to be with the Lord

told me about a touring bus in northern Israel. The road was wet as the bus went around a curve. The heavy vehicle began to slide, and the driver lost control of it. Standing just beside the curve in the road were two children, waiting for the bus. The driver knew the children were in great danger, but they were talking to each other and didn't realize what was happening.

The bus was sliding, and then our pastor called, "Jesus!" It kept sliding. He called again, "Jesus!" The bus kept sliding. The third time he screamed, "Jesus!" Instantly, it seemed as though angels came in front of that bus and held it back. It stopped just before it hit those children. The children's mother came out of her house crying and screaming. She had seen what was happening, but she couldn't have gotten to her children in time. She saw this Scripture proven before her eyes: *"The name of the Lord is a strong tower!"*

> *Every word of God is pure: he is a shield unto them that put their trust in him.*
>
> Proverbs 30:5

We know that every word of God is true and inspired. It is *"pure."* When you love His Word, He becomes your Shield of protection. Don't put your trust in your bank account, your pleasing personal-

ity, your good looks, or your quick humor. Let God
be your *"Shield of protection."*

> *The horse is prepared against the day of battle:*
> *but safety is of the Lord.*   Proverbs 21:31

Don't trust in horses. Don't trust in weapons.
Don't trust in electronic gadgetry. Trust in God. In a
time when horses were used in battle, well-trained
beasts gave their riders an advantage and therefore
lent a certain confidence. But no one is safe outside of
God, for *"safety is of the Lord."*

The Lord desires that we trust and nothing else. In
fact, as we learn wisdom, we should trust Him more:

> *Bow down thine ear, and hear the words of the*
> *wise, and apply thine heart unto my knowledge.*
> *For it is a pleasant thing if thou keep them*
> *within thee; ... That thy trust may be in the*
> *Lord, I have made known to thee this day, even*
> *to thee.*   Proverbs 22:17-19

As we *"bow the ear"* to hear *"the words of the wise,"*
as we *"apply our hearts"* to wisdom's voice, we will
learn to trust in the Lord. We do not seek understanding for its own sake; rather, we allow it to be
our tutor as we mature and grow in our walk and
relationship with the Lord.

5

The Nature of the Sinner

A naughty person, a wicked man, walketh with a froward mouth. He winketh with his eyes, he speaketh with his feet, he teacheth with his fingers; Frowardness is in his heart, he deviseth mischief continually; he soweth discord. Therefore shall his calamity come suddenly; suddenly shall he be broken without remedy.

Proverbs 6:12-15

Proverbs has much to say concerning the nature of sinners, *"the wicked."* This passage describes them and their actions. We should be able to discern the ways of the wicked and we should avoid those ways.

Some of the habits of the wicked described in this passage seem to be minor things. We may think it's harmless to wink our eyes, but it symbolizes deception, and we're not to be deceivers. These may seem like small things, but they're important because a small infection in the body has to be treated, or it doesn't stay small. We can become stumbling blocks to others through the things that we refuse to release to God's care. Therefore, the children of God must learn the ways of the sinner and avoid them.

We may say, "This is my personality," but think about that. When we say that, we're saying we insist on maintaining our old natures. But God wants to reshape us. He wants to form us and mold us, as a potter works his clay. As we become pliant in the hands of the Lord, He will form us into a vessel that will win souls for Him. There must be some reshaping, some pounding, some time in the furnace, but the purpose is that the impurities can be burned out of our lives. The vessel that results will be made to the Lord's design.

Some of the things mentioned in this passage are not so minor. For instance, "froward" describes one who is habitually disobedient, adverse and in opposition to others. We are not to be that way. We are not to be among those who continually seek their own ways, look to their own ease, and oppose any who may come against them. Rather, we are to walk in love, seeking to serve one another.

The differences between the actions and attitudes of the righteous and the wicked are to be abundantly clear to those around us. That is how we become that *"city set on a hill"* whose light simply cannot be hidden.

The *"wicked one"* described in this passage is mischievous. He sows discord. There are Christians who seem to specialize in this area. Churches are being broken apart at an alarming rate. This is not pleasing to God. Splits signal disunity in the Body of Christ. A work which has been destroyed will have to begin again and those who have been involved in church splits may lose their faith. They may become discouraged and do nothing more for God.

The Lord states very clearly how He feels about those who sow discord:

> *These six things doth the LORD hate: yea, seven are an abomination unto Him: ... he that soweth discord among brethren.*
>
> Proverbs 6:16 and 19

Our job as believers is to encourage those around us. We are to battle disunity by building up and strengthening our brothers and sisters. We see this principle of strengthening one another at work in the Old Testament.

At the time of the Babylonian exile, the Lord burdened the heart of Nehemiah for the rebuilding of the wall around Jerusalem. Enemies had come in and broken down the wall so that it lay in ruins. Once Nehemiah, the man of God, had laid hold of the vision of rebuilding the wall, something began to happen. He called the people together and encouraged them, strengthening them in the face of the opposition of their enemies.

Those who hated them came to taunt them as they were rebuilding. They hoped to keep the work of the Lord from continuing. But the people worked together, side by side, and as they worked with one heart, *"in one accord,"* the wall was built. The work was done so quickly that even their enemies had to recognize that it was the Lord who had enabled the builders.

We need to have this attitude. What God has called us to do, we can do. We will fulfill our task with few or with many; but we can do it. And we will strengthen one another to complete the vision. We won't be as the wicked who *"sow discord."*

The wicked not only commit sin; they take delight in it:

> *Who rejoice to do evil, and delight in the fro-*
> *wardness of the wicked.*   Proverbs 2:14

In contrast to this, the righteous are not even to talk about the deeds of the wicked:

> *For it is a shame even to speak of those things*
> *which are done of them in secret.*
> Ephesians 5:12

In our society, with its continual media exposure with movies "based on a true story," which depicts violence and sin masquerading as entertainment, this level of righteousness is almost unheard of. Yet this is our biblical standard: not even to speak of the evil that is committed, not to glory in it or to enjoy hearing of it. Our minds should be on higher things.

The mind of the sinner is on his sin. Sinful thoughts are what he produces. It's as natural as a tree bearing its fruit.

> *The labour of the righteous tendeth to life: the fruit of the wicked to sin.* Proverbs 10:16

Before we came to the Lord, this was also our experience. Our fruit tended toward sin. We couldn't help it. This was simply our natural state. Thank God that through Christ we can be free of our sin, free to live lives pleasing to Him! As He comes to live in our hearts, we no longer have to live bound to sin. He came to set us free from sin. The writer of Hebrews encouraged:

> *Let us lay aside every weight, and the sin which doth so easily beset us, and let us run with patience the race that is set before us.*
>
> Hebrews 12:1

Jesus Himself said:

*If the Son therefore shall make you free, ye shall
be free indeed.*   John 8:36

There are many who still need Christ to set them
free from sin and wickedness, but some who claim to
be Christians already are playing games with God.
They think that because they can get away with certain things in the sight of man, they can do the same
with God. They want to receive the blessings of God,
but not to lay aside their sin in order to achieve it.

Sinners seek personal glory. The Proverbs warn:

*It is not good to eat much honey: so for men to
search their own glory is not glory.*
Proverbs 25:27

Honey is good, but don't eat too much of it or it
will sicken you. And there is nothing wrong with
receiving the praises of men, but be careful. It is not
good to seek your own glory. Exalt Jesus in all things,
giving Him the glory.

At one time we were part of a prison ministry. This
is a very valid ministry, and many people have had
great success for the Gospel in prisons. At one particular prison, however, the inmates, when they gave
testimonies, did not lift up Jesus. They talked about
how they had carried guns, and drunk large
amounts of whiskey, beat their wives, and done

many other terrible things. That could have been the beginning of a great testimony, but they never seemed to get to the part of the story where Jesus laid hold of them and changed their lives. Their testimonies seemed to lack sincerity.

I heard one man say to the prisoner next to him, "I went up for salvation last month. It's your turn." It was just a game to them. But we cannot play games with God. That's why these men were in prison in the first place. They were playing games with themselves and with God, thinking that their sins would not be found out or punished. But they were wrong. They were seeking to glorify themselves.

Proverbs teaches us the need for humility:

> *Put not forth thyself in the presence of the king, and stand not in the place of great men: For better it is that it be said unto thee, Come up hither; than that thou shouldest be put lower in the presence of the prince whom thine eyes have seen.* Proverbs 25:6-7

Left to his own devices, sinful man exalts himself at every turn. Self-exaltation is the nature of the sinner. Humility is the wiser course. Jesus gave a very similar teaching:

> *When thou art bidden of any man to a wedding,*

> *sit not down in the highest room; lest a more*
> *honourable man than thou be bidden of him;*
> *And he that bade thee and him come and say to*
> *thee, Give this man place; and thou begin with*
> *shame to take the lowest room.*   Luke 14:8-9

Taking the "lowest room" doesn't mean that you
will be left there. Humility results in exaltation:

> *But when thou art bidden, go and sit down in*
> *the lowest room; that when he that bade thee*
> *cometh, he may say unto thee, Friend, go up*
> *higher: then shalt thou have worship* [honor] *in*
> *the presence of them that sit at meat with thee.*
>   Luke 14:9-10

As we display godly humility rather than human
pride, we will be exalted ... in God's timing. Jesus
warned:

> *For whosoever exalteth himself shall be abased;*
> *and he that humbleth himself shall be exalted.*
>   Luke 14:11

Humble yourself and let God exalt you. If you try
to exalt yourself, He will have to humble you. So be
willing to do the menial jobs. Be willing to serve your
brothers. Be willing to take a lower seat. This attitude
is pleasing to the Lord, and He will bless you for it.

Not only is natural man proud, but he is also envious. This too is an attitude the Lord wants us to avoid:

> *Wrath is cruel, and anger is outrageous; but who is able to stand before envy?*
>
> Proverbs 27:4

Do you find yourself saying, "I wish I could afford that"? "I wish I were more like him." "I wish I could do that." If so, you need to change your thinking. Be grateful for what you have, not wishful for what you don't have.

We can even be envious of others' ministries or giftings or spiritual abilities. While it is not wrong to want to do more, we may want to be used in a specific ministry, when that is not what the Lord intends for us. Don't let others' abilities and giftings paralyze you into inaction. Never say, "I can't do this," or "I can't do that," but keep in mind what the Bible says:

> *I can do all things through Christ which strengtheneth me.*   Philippians 4:13

A more literal translation of this verse might be, "I can do everything God asks of me through the power of Christ that is resident within me." Whatever God asks us to do, He will enable us to do. We can sur-

vive; we can endure; we can be faithful; we can overcome. We *"can do all things"* that He asks of us.

And why would we want to do anything He is not
wanting us to do? There is no reason for envy. God
has something good for every one of us to do.

"The ways of the wicked" are opposed to the Word of
God. The sinner's ways run contrary to what God
desires for him. Such a one is envious, boastful,
proud, contentious, divisive, and deceitful. Paul
said:

> *Such were some of you: but ye are washed, but*
> *ye are sanctified, but ye are justified in the name*
> *of the Lord Jesus, and by the Spirit of our God.*
> 1 Corinthians 6:11

Let us be grateful to God that He has washed, sanc-
tified, and justified us in the Name of our Lord. And
let's allow Him to give us a burden to draw others
away from the paths of the wicked and to bring them
along with us onto the highway of life in God.

The righteous are truly blessed with the way of life
in Christ. The Bible makes it clear that the wicked
will not prosper:

> *The LORD will not suffer the soul of the righteous*
> *to famish: but he casteth away the substance of*
> *the wicked.*   Proverbs 10:3

A good man leaveth an inheritance to his children's children: and the wealth of the sinner is laid up for the just. Proverbs 13:22

Look carefully at your own soul. *"See if there be any wicked way"* in you. If you want to save your soul from being famished, and cause it to be full of the Word, full of blessing, make sure you are numbered among the righteous. Be diligent to cast aside any unrighteousness the Lord reveals in you. And refuse to walk in *"the ways of the wicked."*

The two ways stand in stark contrast:

The path of the just is as the shining light, that shineth more and more unto the perfect day. The way of the wicked is as darkness: they know not at what they stumble. Proverbs 4:18-19

Shine forth to God's glory!

- 6-

Wisdom in Raising Children

Lo, children are an heritage of the LORD: *and the fruit of the womb is his reward.*   Psalm 127:3

Truly, children are a blessing from the Lord. From the sons of Israel, who multiplied greatly in their bondage, through Sarah, the mother of Isaac, and Hannah, the mother of Samuel, to the woman who ministered to Elisha and was rewarded with a son, we see that children were counted as a gift and a blessing in Old Testament times – at least by those who loved God. This attitude continued in the New Testament accounts as well. Elizabeth rejoiced to find she was with child, even at an advanced age. Mary, of course, was joyous at the birth of her Son. And Jesus healed boys and girls, even raising them from the dead, that the gift of their lives would not be lost.

Today, however, this healthy and godly attitude toward children has been all but lost. Many modern-day Sarahs or Elizabeths would be dismayed at the prospect of childbirth and child-rearing at such an advanced age, and it is not uncommon for younger mothers to view their children as hindrances to their lives and careers. Others view children as accessories to be brought out for admiration when convenient, then put away. Families that have been torn apart by divorce present their own problems, and all too often the children are the ones who suffer most.

The Bible is clear on this matter:

> *Children's children are the crown of old men;*
> *and the glory of children are their fathers.*
>   Proverbs 17:6

Children are a blessing and a *"crown"* of honor. Jesus Himself said, concerning little ones:

> *Suffer* [allow] *little children to come unto me,*
> *and forbid them not: for of such is the kingdom of*
> *God.*   Luke 18:16

Every believer should understand that, according to God's Word, children are to be considered a blessing from the Lord. However, just like other blessings, they come with certain duties and responsibilities.

If the Lord blessed you with a large sum of money that you were not expecting, would you count it your own? Would you immediately spend it on yourself? Or would you count yourself a steward of God's gift and be ready to use it as He directed?

If someone said to you, "I want to bless you and help you to provide food for your family in the coming year. Here is a plot of land, and some seeds, and all things necessary for you to plant and care for your own garden." After you received such a blessing, what would you do? Would you plant the seeds and care for the young plants so you could later reap a harvest? Or would you toss a few seeds into the ground, never weed the garden or care for it in any way, and then be surprised when nothing came of it? How foolish!

When we receive a blessing, be it a prophetic word, a financial gift, or a new-found talent or ability, we need to treasure it, nurture it and use it well. Blessings, although they are often free, bring with them added responsibilities.

The blessing of having children is no different. Parenting is hard work. Parents must provide for their children – spirit, soul, and body. Children need nourishment, shelter, and clothing, but they also need education, instruction, and they need to learn the things of God.

Children can respond to the Lord's invitation to

come to Him. They can worship Him, learn His Word, and have faith to receive His promises, often, it seems, more easily than adults.

The responsibility of parenting also includes providing discipline. Sad to say, this duty has been overlooked in many American homes today. Children seem to be taking over the home, and parents cower before them, realizing that their little ones are "totally out-of-control." This is not what God intended when He created the family. He is a God of order, and He has set a specific order in place for the family. Proverbs has much to say about that order and about the responsibility of parents to discipline their offspring:

> *My son, despise not the chastening of the LORD;*
> *neither be weary of his correction: For whom the*
> *LORD loveth he correcteth; even as a father the*
> *son in whom he delighteth.*   Proverbs 3:11-12

Discipline is not to be despised. It is a sign of love. We correct our children because we love them and want what is best for them. We don't want them to do things that could be harmful, either to themselves or to others. We want them to love the Lord and to have attitudes of obedience and respect toward Him and others.

We see that discipline is to be given in love. It is not

to be done in anger or because a parent happens to be in a bad mood. Discipline is to be meted out with a clear mind and with consistency. Ideally, the boundaries should be clear, and the results of disobedience should also be clear.

> *He that spareth his rod hateth his son: but he*
> *that loveth him chasteneth him betimes.*
>
> Proverbs 13:24

This is one of the most urgent lessons of our time. Many people all over the Earth have adopted the attitude that children know best and have allowed the children of the family to keep everyone in tyranny. This is not God's plan. Allowing the child to control the household only makes both the child and the parents miserable. God will hold parents accountable for their unwillingness to discipline their children.

A child who is not disciplined grows up as a stubborn, rebellious and self-willed person. This is a major problem in our world today. We have too many selfish adults who have never learned self-discipline; for isn't that one of the goals of parental discipline?

While it is wrong to take out one's anger and frustration with life on a child — for that type of action too often becomes abuse rather than discipline and often has a permanent psychological impact on the child — it is equally wrong to offer no discipline at all. Both of these responses are a serious misuse of the blessing that God intended children to be. God's way is the best way in all things.

We may not want to discipline our children. After all, it takes work and effort, especially if we're to be consistent. And most children fail to appreciate our efforts at the time. How could they? But discipline is necessary. If we deal with the problems in children's lives when they are still small, we won't have to deal with those problems later in life, when they all too often become serious problems. If we don't do anything now, the problem won't go away; it will grow.

This isn't just an American problem. We've seen it in many other countries. Mothers sometimes bring us their sons when we minister there, saying, "I can't do a thing with him." Well, if the parent can't do anything with a fourteen- or fifteen-year-old child, I can't either. What these parents are really saying is that they never did exercise control over their child. They didn't start soon enough. If a young teenager has never been corrected in his lifetime, it's a little late to start now. They will probably abuse drugs and show disrespect for authority and they just might end up in jail or worse. Unruly teenagers have all sorts of problems. They don't know anything about self-discipline. And how could they? They have never been disciplined, but have done just what they wanted.

The Scriptures are clear:

> *Chasten thy son while there is hope, and let not thy soul spare for his crying.* Proverbs 19:18

When is there "hope"? Usually, while the child is still young. Children should grow up walking in discipline, learning to obey their parents and to have respect for those in authority over them. They should learn self-discipline, and this will enable them to become responsible people.

If we listen to what children are saying, if our *"souls spare for his crying,"* we become too lenient, and while there is a place for grace and mercy in disciplining our children, permissive parenting is not really loving parenting. Children will always test the limits we set, and always want us to be more lenient, but they will be more secure when they know where those limits lie and happier when they are required to live within them.

Many people today have the idea that discipline drives your children away from you, but that is just the opposite of the truth. Godly discipline can bring parents and children closer together.

Discipline must always be meted out in love, whether it be a spanking or a withdrawal of privileges. As our children see our love, and the consistency with which we work toward helping them to become mature, responsible men and women of God, they will be drawn closer to us because we care enough to help them to do what is right.

Teenage crime has risen at an alarming rate in our society. Alcohol or other drug abuse is also a factor. Even in some small towns there is evidence of hate crimes and gang-related violence. Children, left to their own devices, will not grow up into strong, healthy citizens. They need our help. *"Spare not ... for his crying."* The results of hands-off child rearing has led to a troubled society.

Those who lack discipline often fail spiritually, and children who are undisciplined often grow into indisciplined adults. Prayer, Bible study, biblical meditation, and ministering to others all require self-discipline. Don't hesitate to give it. It will *"give wisdom"* and a lack of it will bring *"shame"*:

> *The rod and reproof give wisdom: but a child left*
> *to himself bringeth his mother to shame.*
>
> Proverbs 29:15

Even adults occasionally need to be disciplined, and the Lord shows us His love by administering proper discipline to our lives. If God left us to our own devices, we would grow up like weeds. But He loves us and wants us to grow into responsible people. If you live as you want and do what you think is right, you will end up in trouble. God can't allow that without trying to help you, so He corrects you and He expects you to correct your children. Guidance and correction are not intended just to cause pain, but their purpose is to *"give wisdom."*

We must train our children, not just to be "good people," but to be righteous men and women of God:

> *Train up a child in the way he should go: and when he is old, he will not depart from it.*
>
> Proverbs 22:6

This is a wonderful promise, but it is for those who fulfill its requirements. All the promises found in the Scriptures have such conditions. If we come into line with the Word of God, nothing can prevent us from having His promised blessings in our lives.

We can raise our children to be men and women of God, mature believers who love the Lord. That doesn't mean that a child will never stray from the way of the Lord. It doesn't mean that he will never get into any trouble. Each child grows into an individual and must make his own decisions about right living and about serving God. But as we are faithful to pray for our children and to train them in righteousness, the Lord will honor our efforts and put

His hand on our children. Pray for your children, and God will use them for His glory.

The conduct of a child always reflects on his parents, and we can usually see by his actions whether or not a child is being disciplined at home:

> *Even a child is known by his doings, whether his work be pure, and whether it be right.*
>
> Proverbs 20:11

We all want the very best for our children, and we want them to bring glory to God. We should be grateful that He loved us enough to give us the privilege of raising them and of helping them to become all that He intended them to be. We know that God has a plan for each of us, including our children, and disciplining them in the biblical way can help them to fulfill God's purpose in life.

Most important of all, we must be examples to our children. They should be able to see in our lives those things we say we believe in. Our children are our first sphere of ministry. We are to draw them to Christ, and to lives that are marked by purity, integrity, and the love of the Lord. We should be able to say to our children, as Paul said to the Corinthian church:

> *Be ye followers of me, even as I also am of Christ.*
>
> 1 Corinthians 11:1

When we are living our lives as examples of godliness for our children to follow, then they will come to know the fear of the Lord. As we reflect the life and the love of the Lord to the children He has graciously placed in our care, we are parenting in wisdom. God will bless such parenting, and the result will be blessed children.

7

Righteous Living

The fining pot is for silver, and the furnace for gold: but the LORD trieth the hearts.

Proverbs 17:3

The Lord is in the refining business, but He is not interested in the metals we call "precious." He's more interested in what He sees as precious – our hearts. His plan and desire is that we come forth as pure silver and gold. He wants to refine us, so that we have no impurities or defects. We are to be righteous, holy, set apart for Him. That refining process takes two things: heat and pressure. Purity comes forth in the fire.

A normal fire is not enough for a refiner of silver and gold. He also uses pressure. Ouch! Fire is hot and pressure is hard to bear, but the combination of the fire and pressure produces the finest and purest gold and silver.

God has put you into His pressure cooker to prepare you for His glory. He wants you to be as pure
gold. But don't worry. He won't use more pressure
or more heat than is absolutely necessary. Trust Him.
Too much heat or pressure will damage or destroy a
substance. God knows when the heat or the pressure
is just enough for us. He knows what you can bear.

"Oh, Lord," we cry out, "the pressure is more than
I can bear!"

"No," He answers, "you're wrong. I know what
you can bear, and this fire needs to be about twenty
degrees hotter to bring out the best in your spirit."

Oh, thank God, He knows us, and we can surely
trust His wisdom. He is working *"righteousness"* in
us.

Proverbs has much to say concerning *righteousness*
and *righteous living,* but these are not terms that we
hear much in everyday English. What exactly do
they mean? *Righteousness* means "conforming to a
standard of right and justice." Paul taught us:

> *And be not conformed to this world: but be ye*
> *transformed by the renewing of your mind, that*
> *ye may prove what is that good, and acceptable,*
> *and perfect, will of God.*   Romans 12:2

The standard of this world is flawed, but the standard of the Lord is perfect. We must, therefore, be

transformed by His power so that we can be like Him.

When we discover, as we often do, that we are not totally conformed to the image of Christ and sin is found in us, what should be our response? Proverbs wisely teaches:

> *He that covereth his sins shall not prosper: but whoso confesseth and forsaketh them shall have mercy.* Proverbs 28:13

Confessing sin and forsaking it should go together. God requires that we both recognize that we have done wrong, confess it to Him, and that we forsake it. Confession is not enough. God requires that you begin a new life, forsaking the old. If you admit your wrong but keep repeating it over and over, that cannot be pleasing to God. Forsake it. Turn away from it. Not only that, but turn away from bad companions. Turn away from those places and things that bring you into temptation.

If certain types of music, or books, or magazines, or television programs tempt you or cause you to sin, stay away from them. Why risk losing your anointing? Why risk losing your very soul?

If you try to hide your wrong, you won't prosper. If you try to make excuses for your sin, you won't grow in God. Confess it and forsake it. That is the only way to righteousness and purity. And the alternative is not pleasing:

> *Whoso walketh uprightly shall be saved: but he*
> *that is perverse in his ways shall fall at once.*
>   Proverbs 28:18

A perverse — obstinate, hardheaded, stubborn or rebellious — person is not pleasing to God. His perversity will cause him to fall, and quickly. This is not necessarily due to the judgment of God, but is the natural outcome of perverse living.

The word *"saved"* in this verse does not speak only of a spiritual salvation. It conveys the total sense of the word: saved from enemies, saved from sickness, saved from dangers; fully, totally saved in every way. This is the promise to those who walk uprightly. What is the path of those who walk in righteousness?

> *The highway of the upright is to depart from*
> *evil: he that keepeth his way preserveth his soul.*
>   Proverbs 16:17

Are you continually departing from evil when the opportunity presents itself? Are you growing in holiness, in righteousness, in your walk with God? Are you hungering and thirsting for God, and for what

He has for you to do and to be? Then you are on the *"highway of the upright."* That highway of holiness, that pathway to Heaven is the place we should all want to be, growing closer and closer to Jesus as the days go by, striving to gain His favor and be established in Him:

> *A good man obtaineth favour of the LORD: but a man of wicked devices will he condemn. A man shall not be established by wickedness: but the root of the righteous shall not be moved.*
>
> Proverbs 12:2-3

God has promised enduring blessing to the righteous. In order to stay in this way of righteousness, we must call upon His strength day by day and depend fully upon His Word. Speak it forth, believe it, and put it into action.

It may appear, at times, that the wicked are being established rather than the righteous, but that is a deception. The prosperity of the wicked is not lasting. When we stand in God's righteousness, we can declare, "I shall not be moved," and nothing Satan can do will move us.

> *The thoughts of the righteous are right: but the counsels of the wicked are deceit.*
>
> Proverbs 12:5

We should be careful not to entrust ourselves to worldly people. Their motives are not pure. They may be deceitful or they may be deceived. Either way, we cannot trust in their counsel. Be very careful about taking advice from those who don't know God.

God has placed His righteous thoughts, His wisdom, within us. These are the thoughts that we must be projecting through our conversations.

How can we know that our thoughts conform to God's standards? If our thoughts are of fear or of discouragement, they are not of Him. If our thoughts disregard or violate the teachings of His holy Word, they are not of Him.

We must fill ourselves with His Word, so that our thoughts begin to conform more fully to His. Then we shall be better able to stand in God.

> *The wicked are overthrown, and are not: but the house of the righteous shall stand.*
>
> Proverbs 12:7

Through every storm we face in this life, whether it be physical or spiritual, emotional or financial, a storm in our relationships or in our job situations, we can rest assured that our house *"shall stand."* Everything around us may be falling. The winds may be blowing with such ferocity that there seems to be no hope, but because we are established on the Rock, we will not be moved. We have a more excellent way:

> *The righteous is more excellent than his neighbour: but the way of the wicked seduceth them.*
>
> Proverbs 12:26

"The righteous is more excellent than his neighbour." What a wonderful promise! We can project excellence, we can overcome adversity and show forth the nature of Christ to the world, when we are willing to walk in righteousness.

When you live righteously, people will see something different about you. When you walk righteously, people will recognize the divine in your life. Righteous people treat their families differently. Righteous people treat their neighbors differently. Righteous people are loving and kind, helpful and honest. They make themselves available to help those who are in need. They are *"more excellent."*

> *The wicked desireth the net of evil men: but the root of the righteous yieldeth fruit.*
>
> Proverbs 12:12

God's people are to be fruit producers. This is part of our *"more excellent"* life. The fruit of the Spirit should be evident in us.

Paul also compared the way of the world and the ways of the righteous:

> *Now the works of the flesh are manifest, which are these; Adultery, fornication, uncleanness, lasciviousness, Idolatry, witchcraft, hatred, variance, emulations, wrath, strife, seditions, heresies, Envyings, murders, drunkenness, revellings, and such like: of the which I tell you before, as I have also told you in time past, that they which do such things shall not inherit the kingdom of God.*   Galatians 5:19-21

There are many more works of the flesh than Paul could mention so he added *"such like"* to cover the rest, yet there are only nine fruits of the Spirit. But, if we are determined to show forth righteousness, it doesn't matter how many evils there are in the world. The fruits of the Spirit are more than sufficient to overcome all the deeds of flesh. God's people have never depended on superiority in numbers. They depend on God, on His power and His authority.

The fruit of the Spirit is the result of righteous living. These fruit are borne in our lives as we learn to put our trust in God, and as we put into action the wisdom He gives.

> *But the fruit of the Spirit is love, joy, peace,*

> *longsuffering, gentleness, goodness, faith,*
> *Meekness, temperance: against such there is no*
> *law.* Galatians 5:22-23

"The root of the righteous yieldeth fruit." This is the kind of fruit we want to produce in our lives, and to share with others. This fruit produces life, another of the blessings God has prepared for the righteous:

> *In the way of righteousness is life; and in the*
> *pathway thereof there is no death.*
> Proverbs 12:28

What more could we ask? Because Jesus is Life, those who live for Him have life. Nothing could be simpler. He offers life and *"life more abundantly,"* both here on the Earth and for all eternity. *"There is no death"* in this pathway. Praise God!

Death represents, for most people, their greatest fear. But death has no hold over us when we live in Jesus. He has the keys of death. So it pays to conform to the standard of right and justice. It brings us life and takes away the fear of death.

When we want to measure our lives and see how we are doing in the matter of righteousness, we must not compare ourselves with others. We must measure ourselves against God's standard of right and justice, His righteousness. God's requirements do not change depending on who you are. They do not change depending on your status in life. They simply do not change. They are the same for everyone. We cannot ask God to make an exception in our case. We must decide to measure up to His standard.

If you want to pass the Board Examination to become a lawyer or a medical doctor or a dentist, you cannot expect the Board to make an exception in your case and to accept your excuses as to why you are justified in not fully complying with their requirements. You either measure up to the established standard or you don't. No matter what the excuse, if you don't pass the Board exam, you will not be approved for service in your chosen field of endeavor.

God has placed a very high standard of conduct upon those who will be called His children. Forget your personal concepts of righteousness, and start living up to the standard God has established. Our standard of conduct must be in keeping with the standard laid down in the Bible, God's Word.

In a simpler sense, righteous living is just living in a way that pleases our Heavenly Father. Jesus set an example for us. He was a Man of prayer, of fasting, of meditation. If He was busy ministering to the needs of people throughout the day, He spent the night in prayer with God. He was a Man of the Word who knew well the promises of God. He was a Man of obedience, faithful to do what the Father instructed Him. Most of all, Jesus loved people and responded to their needs wherever He went.

So if you want to please God, don't be too weary to minister to people around you. Someone may be ready to commit suicide. Someone may be near death. Someone may be experiencing his last opportunity in life. Don't rob him of that chance to be set free. If God leads you to bless someone, don't put it off until tomorrow. Work righteousness today. There may be no opportunity tomorrow. Give of yourself, and God will give you grace to continue.

God has called us to be a blessing, not to beat people down. After teaching in a particular home meeting one evening, one of those who was present said to us, "It was such a blessing not to be criticized and judged and condemned." People in the church have been beaten down long enough. They don't need more of that. They need to be comforted and encouraged and loved. That is God's way.

Christ showed this way when He was confronted by the Pharisees with the woman taken in adultery. He could have said, "Well, let's go out and stone her like the Word says." But He didn't. He said, "This is a new day, and I have got a new commandment for you: Love." That's not only what Jesus said. That's what Jesus is, for *"God is love"* (1 John 4:8). We must show the world His love and His mercy, allowing them to see His righteousness in our lives.

As Christians, it isn't always easy to make the choice to do what's right. We all have a human tendency toward sin. We all struggle with the sin nature. But no one forces us to sin. Although there is temptation, we can overcome it.

Young people have sometimes told me that temptation is just too great in their lives, but that cannot be true. It contradicts what God has said. He said that although our temptations would be great, He would *"make a way to escape"*:

> *There hath no temptation taken you but such as is common to man: but God is faithful, who will not suffer you to be tempted above that ye are able; but will with the temptation also make a way to escape, that ye may be able to bear it.*
>
> 1 Corinthians 10:13

To the Apostle Paul, God said:

> *My grace is sufficient for thee: for my strength is made perfect in weakness. Most gladly therefore will I rather glory in my infirmities, that the power of Christ may rest upon me.*
>
> 2 Corinthians 12:9

There is grace for each of us. Just reach out for it. If you were drowning, going down for the third time, you would certainly reach out for any help offered to you. So if you are going down spiritually, you must reach out for God. Jesus is there, always reaching out for you. Receive the grace He offers you.

You have great promises from God:

*For the upright shall dwell in the land, and the
perfect shall remain in it.*   Proverbs 2:21

"The upright." I hope that's you, so that you can
"dwell in the land."

We are about to see some great changes in the
Earth. God will restore His creation to a state of purity. Once, when I was in Tibet, God spoke to me
specifically about that time and about what He
would do. "I will restore this world to its former
state," He said. I am excited about what God will do
here on the Earth and I want to be sure that I am in a
position to be part of it. He is looking for those who
will be qualified to help Him accomplish His purposes on the Earth. He is looking for a mature and
responsible people. He is looking for people who
will say, "Anything You want, Lord, I'll do it. I'm
available." That is the prayer of the upright. That is
the response of those who will "dwell in the land."

Let us be those who follow after righteousness.
Then we will bless the Lord, we will bless others, and
we ourselves will be blessed.

*He that followeth after righteousness and mercy
findeth life, righteousness, and honour.*
                                    Proverbs 21:21

8

True and False Riches

There is that maketh himself rich, yet hath noth-ing: there is that maketh himself poor, yet hath great riches.   Proverbs 13:7

This proverb seems preposterous, but it is true. The Apostle Paul wrote:

As sorrowful, yet alway rejoicing; as poor, yet making many rich; as having nothing, and yet possessing all things.   2 Corinthians 6:10

It makes no sense whatsoever to the natural mind that a poor person can actually be rich, but God counts riches in a totally different way than we do. He knows what has real and lasting value.

God wants us, His people, to be rich, not so that we can heap up possessions and allow our souls to wither, but so that we can have the things we need in life and so that we can use our resources for His glory. But there are things much more important than houses and lands and cars and jewelry and stocks and bonds, and God calls them "riches." We must learn to labor for that which will not perish.

The riches of this world cannot satisfy. They cannot bring us peace. We must learn to depend on God, not on our checkbooks or our savings or our jobs. If we always look to what we can see, we are limited. If we never learn to look to God, we limit what He can do for us. Trust Him, and let Him receive all the glory.

God said of those who concentrate on making themselves rich: *"He hath nothing."* In other countries, we are often invited to stay in the homes of people of considerable means, but we soon find that those people have serious problems that many of the poor could never imagine. Proverbs declares:

> *Better is the poor that walketh in his uprightness* [or integrity], *than he that is perverse in his ways, though he be rich.*   Proverbs 28:6

Most people, if given the choice, would rather be rich than poor. My personal goal at one time was to build up as much treasure as I could in this world. But natural riches don't automatically bring blessings and joy. It is better to be poor and upright than to be rich and have nothing of value. God wants the very best for His people. He knows how to bless us materially when He wants. And He will.

A poor man who has integrity is better off than a rich man who is perverse. Still, better yet is a man of integrity who knows how to maintain his integrity and prosper.

There can be no doubt that prosperity is God's will for us. He said:

> *Beloved, I wish above all things that thou mayest prosper and be in health, even as thy soul prospereth.*   3 John 2

But we can prosper and still remain honest. We can prosper and still remain holy. We can prosper and still remain upright.

Ask God to help you handle riches — for His glory. If you are willing to use your finances for His glory and purpose, He can take the limits off of your financial life and give you all that is necessary to perform His will in your life. We will see more about handling riches properly in the following chapter.

One of the most important lessons we all need to learn, in order to prosper, is how to give to God. When I was young in the Lord, I was great at holding onto my money. When an offering was taken, I held my money as tightly as I could so that as little as possible would escape. What I didn't realize was that if I didn't get that seed into the ground, I couldn't reap a harvest. When I finally learned to give, the Lord blessed my giving and caused it to grow into a blessing, for me and for others. Then I was sorry for the times I had held back. I hadn't known what I was missing.

God is so wonderful. He supplies our every need. His blessing makes us rich:

> *The tongue of the just is AS CHOICE SILVER: the heart of the wicked is little worth. The lips of the righteous FEED MANY: but fools die for want of wisdom. The blessing of the Lord, it MAKETH RICH, and He addeth no sorrow with it.*   Proverbs 10:20-22

"He addeth no sorrow." The mad rush for riches often leaves people emotionally devastated. But when we are financially blessed of God, spiritual blessing comes with it. We serve a God of miracles and provision. His ways bring no sorrow or pain. There is no fear or depression attached with seeking God's ways. If we walk with Him, we need not experience those things. Step into the positive where God's blessings will flow in your life.

God wants to make us rich. The riches He gives may or may not be what the world would call "riches," but He knows best. And He desires that we learn to use what He puts in our hands in a way that is pleasing to Him.

He will give us the finances we need to further the Gospel and spread His Word to the nations. We must take advantage of open doors since we don't know how long they might remain open.

God is a generous Giver, and the riches He puts in our hands, tangible and intangible, are wonderful and to be treasured. I'm rich because God has given me a treasure in the form of my wife and children. They have been a wonderful blessing to me through the years. Such relationships are treasures. Friendships are treasures. Abilities and talents and skills – artistic talents or musical talents, for example – are all treasures. Learn to treasure and appreciate every rich blessing from God.

Wisdom and understanding are treasures from God:

> *For the merchandise of it* [wisdom and understanding] *is better than the merchandise of silver, and the gain thereof than fine gold. She is more precious than rubies: and all the things thou canst desire are not to be compared unto her.* Proverbs 3:14

These are among the true riches and, as this proverb indicates, are to be valued more than *"silver and ... fine gold."* Silver and gold, here, are symbolic of all earthly riches. They represent money or real estate or stocks or mines or any other valuable commodity, and wisdom is to be valued above them all. *"All the things thou canst desire"* seems to include anything of value that we could possibly think of. Yet wisdom is so much greater in value that it is *"not to be compared."*

Each of us has a different value system and, therefore, hold things in varying degrees of respect. We all have certain things that are very precious to us. There are certain things that we hold very tightly and are loathe to think of giving up. These are often the very things God requires of us. If we are willing to give God what He asks of us, we will surely be blessed. He will open up the treasures of Heaven and pour out great blessings upon us.

When I had my dental business, I was able to provide well for my wife and children. After I came to know the Lord more deeply, I heard His say to me one day, "I want to care for you and your family." And His care has proved to be wonderful. He is our Provider.

True riches accompany wisdom:

Length of days is in her right hand; and in her

left hand riches and honour. Her ways are ways
of pleasantness, and all her paths are peace.

Proverbs 3:16-17

"Length of days."
"Riches."
"Honor."
"Pleasantness."
"Peace."

That's a pretty impressive list. What good things
God gives us when we seek His wisdom and understanding!

Why should we chase after the false riches of this
world and miss the good things of God? His riches
do not corrupt the hearts of men and turn them away
from the truth. His riches do not rob us of the important things in life. They are the important things in
life.

Often, when we are speaking about the things of
God, we call them "the precious things of God," and
they are precious. If we fail to value these things, we
are mistaken and will suffer the consequences. They
are "precious things" to those who love God and call
upon His Name.

When we speak about God's Word, we often say
"the precious Word of God," and it is precious. We
meditate on it, consider it, lay hold of it and put it to
work in our lives. The more we can get of God, the

less we will have of our old nature, so, through fasting and prayer and meditation upon the Word of God, we take on more of His holiness and less of our worldliness. Before long, the way we used to be, the attitudes that we used to have, and the personality we used to display are all things of the past. More of Him and less of us. As John the Baptist put it:

He must increase, but I must decrease.
                                                    John 3:30

The attitude of the world is exactly the opposite. Men and women grow up to believe that they must pull themselves up in life and if they don't do it, it won't be done. But when we lose ourselves in God and His goodness, we find the truly valuable and important things in life.

Men of the world desire to increase financially or to develop their personality, so that they will be noticed by others. Hiding themselves in God would seem to be the last thing they would ever want to do. But when we willingly choose to hide ourselves in Him, it is a delight to see what He can make of us.

Learn to be satisfied with what God does in your life. Thank Him for what He has already done and for what He plans to do in the future. Position yourself to continue to grow and to receive from God, and your success in the future will be assured.

Allow the Lord to work in your life. Be attentive to Him, and walk in humility so that He can add to you all the things that He has prepared for your life. His adding will not be so that others will recognize and appreciate you but so that you can minister to others what God has entrusted to you – whether it be money, wisdom, or something else.

Receiving the riches of God requires that you empty yourself of self. He must receive all the glory. If a vessel is full nothing can be added to it. It you are full of yourself, how can God pour His goodness into you? We must decrease so that He can increase.

Decreasing may be a bit uncomfortable sometimes, but when we realize that the purpose is not to make us feel badly or to consider ourselves as having somehow diminished, we will gladly submit and reap the benefits. God knows how to produce gold in every one of us – if we will let Him do it.

Seeking God's riches turns everything on its ear, and our motives are totally changed. The Proverbs insists:

> *Labour not to be rich: cease from thine own wisdom.*   Proverbs 23:4

Our human wisdom tells us to build up vast earthly treasures, but God's wisdom tells us not to do that, to work with another motivation. Human wisdom tells us, "Save, and what you save you'll have; give, and what you give away is gone." I was taught that, and many of us were. It took me a long time to realize that God had a very different way of doing things. In God's economy, giving brings a release. It blesses both the person who is receiving the gift and the giver who is obeying God in giving it.

Money is a powerful motivation for people. They will do most anything for it. It is not uncommon for people to work two jobs, making great personal sacrifices to earn more. Many of those same people would never make those same sacrifices to achieve spiritual success. In many nations of the world people work six and a half or even seven days a week, to somehow have a better life and a secure future.

Capitalism and democracy have given the people of many lands the freedom to determine their own future and the freedom to live as they want today. The sad thing is that many people who are supposed to be free are not free at all. They are slaves to their lust for money. And this is true of the most prosperous nations on Earth.

Many of the products we use in America come from countries where people work under conditions that we would consider to be substandard, very much like a sweatshop. Yet these people are happy to have the work and don't consider their place of work to be a sweatshop at all.

The freedom to create wealth can become a terrible bondage in itself and we must be careful not to fall into the trap of seeking wealth for wealth's sake. There are many more important things in life. We need money, but we must not be controlled by it.

How about you? Are you guilty of pursuing false riches? Do you work solely for things that are destined to perish, rather than for eternal values? Take inventory of your life today.

> *Remove far from me vanity and lies: give me neither poverty nor riches; feed me with food convenient for me: Lest I be full, and deny thee, and say, Who is the LORD? or lest I be poor, and steal, and take the name of my God in vain.*
>
> Proverbs 30:8-9

These are the words of a wise man, a man inspired of God. He is asking the Lord to give him the proper attitude concerning wealth. He wants neither too much nor too little, lest his heart sin toward the Lord. He prays, "Don't give me more than I need, for I might not be able to handle it. I might think, *Why do I need the Lord? I am full. I am satisfied. Why should I pray? I have no needs. I have no concerns.* Lord, don't allow that to happen to me. Let my heart be right before You.

"And don't allow me to be in want, lest I sin

against You. Help me to keep my heart and actions pure in this matter."

If you have pure motives in everything you do, money will not spoil you and prosperity will not do you harm. Do nothing in life purely for monetary reward. Work for eternal things and store up riches that will last throughout eternity.

9

The Benefits of a Generous Spirit

He that oppresseth the poor to increase his riches, and he that giveth to the rich, shall surely come to want. Proverbs 22:16

We are not here to oppress, but to bless. We are also not here to lavish all that comes our way on ourselves. Sometimes we Americans have an attitude that says, "When I have plenty for myself, I will give what is left over to bless others." Too often we seem to be like the foolish man described by Jesus. When the Lord had blessed him with an abundance of crops, his immediate thought was not to feed the poor or to bless others, but to build bigger barns to keep everything for himself. God said he was a *"fool"*:

But God said unto him, Thou fool, this night thy

*soul shall be required of thee: then whose shall
those things be, which thou hast provided? So is
he that layeth up treasures for himself, and is not
rich toward God.*   Luke 12:20-21

It is not wrong to have treasures. Indeed God
wants to give them to each of us, but we must learn
to handle them, or they can destroy us. We must
learn to lay up treasures in Heaven, and be *"rich toward God."* This generous and wise spirit was
exemplified by a friend of ours, Enoch Nelson, a pio-
neer missionary from Ontario, Canada. Enoch went
out to the mission field when he was fifty-five, about
the time most people start thinking of retirement. He
was not well physically, but because he was willing
to go out ill, God caused him to come home well.

Because of his age, no mission society would support Enoch, so he went out to eastern and central
Africa, trusting God to supply for him. Traveling
from village to village in the interior areas, he
preached the Word of God and raised up disciples.
He developed a sort of walking Bible school. Today,
thirty years after the fact, the churches that he established in this way are still in operation. Enoch Nelson
is a rich man.

We can learn from people like that. God will bless
those who give Him the opportunity to do so. You
can reach out and bless others – if you are willing to

concentrate on spiritual riches. If you insist on focusing on natural things, you will lose in the end:

> *He that hath a bountiful eye shall be blessed; for he giveth of his bread to the poor.*
>
> Proverbs 22:9

The love of Christ causes us to want to love and bless others, and the wonderful thing is that we lose nothing by being generous with those in need. When you see others whose need is greater than yours, bless them. You lose nothing, for God will send those who have more than you to bless you. We all feel the need of something, but no matter how great your personal need, you can always find someone with a greater need.

Having *"a bountiful eye"* means that you look for ways to bless people. You become sensitive to the needs of those around you. But in this, as in all things, we must be careful to listen to what God wants us to do.

One of the problems we encounter these days is that there are so many ministries competing for the available funds. We all receive many requests for particular needs. In this case, the only right thing to do is to pray and ask God to help you make the proper decision. It takes the wisdom of God to make the right decision about giving. Don't dismiss requests outright, as many do. And don't automatically give, as others do. Listen to the voice of God in regard to your giving. Let God show you His heart. Let Him show you His people. Let Him show you His projects.

We need to have *"a bountiful eye"* wherever we go, remaining sensitive to what the Lord is saying to us. A few years ago Ginny and I traveled to Brazil and ministered there for two months. As we were leaving the Lord told us not to take any of the money we had received in offerings from various churches and individuals out of the country.

My first thought was, "Well, I had to pay for our airline tickets to get us here. Nobody sent us an invitation complete with airfare." People hadn't even known us, yet God had told us to go there. Now He was telling us to leave behind the offerings we had received. As I prayed, I sensed that it was because there were many people there whose needs were greater than our own. And we lost nothing by being generous to them.

When we first began traveling to other countries many years ago, it didn't take long for us to discover how very much we had in terms of material wealth, by comparison with the people we met. It was our joy to learn to bless other people.

Those who have *"bountiful eye[s]"* look for ways to

bless others. We start thinking, *How can I bless this person? How can I encourage that ministry?* Our concern is no longer with what we can receive, but with what we can give to others. This is the way of wisdom, and the attitude that pleases the Lord:

> *He that giveth unto the poor shall not lack: but he that hideth his eyes shall have many a curse.*
> Proverbs 28:27

There was a period in the early development of our country when people who had no stable means of supporting themselves and no family to support them wound up in the "poor house." What a dreadful, humiliating experience that must have been! Thank God we no longer have poor houses in America. We now have generous government assistance programs. Our country has been generous and generous people need never fear. You *"shall not lack"* is the promise of God.

If we pretend not to see the needs of those around us, God's promise is not pleasant: *"many a curse."* When the Lord speaks to you about giving, never turn a deaf ear. Never be guilty of saying, "I have already given once."

God wants to bless and enlarge you, so He gives you the opportunity to bless others and to bless His work. Don't hesitate to give.

*He that despiseth his neighbour sinneth: but he
that hath mercy on the poor, happy is he.*

Proverbs 14:21

Jesus was our example. He never disparaged the
poor. He loved them and gave His life for them. He
didn't tell us to forget the poor or to turn our backs
on them. And He certainly didn't tell us to pretend
that they didn't exist. You will be happy if you have
"mercy on the poor."

There is an incentive for Christians to minister to
poor people, for they often listen more readily to the
Gospel than do the rich. The rich have need of nothing, but the poor readily recognize their needs. Being
poor and being poorly educated do not necessarily
go together, but they often do, and simple people
believe more readily. They don't have to overcome
their intellect. This is one of the reasons it is so enjoy-
able to preach in the Third World countries: the
people are so open to the Gospel. Many rich people
have hardened their hearts against God's message or
just don't have time to listen to it.

This doesn't mean that God has forgotten the rich.
Not at all! He cares about rich people just as much as
He does about poor people and hasn't forgotten
them in any sense. It pleases Him when those who
are prosperous remember Him, as well, and give to
His work, making the task of building the Kingdom

of God much easier. Giving to the needs of ministries is giving to God:

> *He that hath pity upon the poor lendeth unto the Lord; and that which he hath given will he pay him again.* Proverbs 19:17

Giving to needy ventures is an investment into the Kingdom of God and God is faithful to repay those who invest in His Kingdom. Not all giving is wise giving:

> *He that oppresseth the poor to increase his riches, and he that giveth to the rich, shall surely come to want.* Proverbs 22:16

The rich don't need your money. They have enough already. And the poor don't need your oppression. They have enough already. Giving to the rich and oppressing the poor is the way of the world. Once you are in Christ, you must learn to know His voice and to feel His heart. He has compassion on the needy of this world and will move on you to help them too.

Many poor people don't seem to be worthy of our help. When we walk in the Spirit, however, we are not guided by how someone dresses or where they are from. We learn to obey God, regardless of people's appearances.

When Jesus was on Earth, some men asked, "Can any good thing come out of Nazareth?" So the town where Jesus was born didn't have a very good reputation. The world continues to judge people by the circumstances of their lives: where they come from or who their family is or how much education they have had. But God looks upon the heart:

> For the Lord seeth not as man seeth; for man
> looketh on the outward appearance, but the LORD
> looketh on the heart.   1 Samuel 16:7

This is not to say that we should just give to everyone for every cause. We could easily give all our money away, and then, when the Lord spoke to us about a particular need, we would be powerless to respond. We must be wise in our giving.

We must also be ready to receive, so that others can be blessed, as well. Many years ago, Ginny and I traveled to the Bahamas for ministry. Some of our best times there were preaching along the boardwalks in Nassau. We were located in a park just in front of the place where some eleven or twelve cruise ships docked, and we often saw rich tourists disembark. For the most part, those rich tourists ignored our little group. Nearby were some vendors, ladies who made straw hats and purses to sell to the tourists, and many of them were blessed by our ministry there. I remember one lady turning around and giving me an offering of $5.00.

I was startled and said to myself, "I can't take that." I was still in my dental practice and doing well financially. But God showed me that the gift the lady was offering was for her blessing, not mine, so I received it and was glad. If I am blessed because I give to others, others can be blessed by giving to me. So I must be open to that.

When we have a proper attitude toward money, we never come to trust it:

> *He that trusteth in his riches shall fall: but the righteous shall flourish as a branch.*
>
> Proverbs 11:28

Any man who trusts in riches will fall, no matter how much he might have. Money can be stolen. Unexpected sicknesses can cause huge expenditures. The government may want a larger share than you'd planned on. Many things can happen. Don't trust in your money. Trust in God, for *"the righteous shall flourish."*

When I sold my business and the building in which it was housed, the Lord told me exactly what price I was to get for it, and I got it. The Lord told me to give Him what was His, to buy an airline ticket, and to put the rest of the money in the bank to use as He would direct me in the coming days. I obeyed.

My wife and I began to travel with our pastor on ministry trips abroad. We went to China four times, to Russia, and to many other places. And each of those trips cost us thousands of dollars.

One day the Lord said to me, "You're living off your bank account, aren't you?"

I said, "Yes, I am."

He said, "What do you notice about that account?"

I said, "It's going down fast."

"As your bank account goes down," the Lord said, "I want your faith in Me to increase. Then, when your bank account gets down to zero, and you have exhausted all your savings, I will supply all your needs." And that's exactly what happened.

God will do the same thing for you, if you put your faith in Him and not in bank accounts.

Some people insist on interpreting all the Bible verses that refer to prosperity as a spiritual prosperity. We do want and expect that spiritual prosperity, but there can be no doubt that God wants us to prosper materially as well. And no one can steal those blessings from us:

> *Whoso causeth the righteous to go astray in an evil way, he shall fall himself into his own pit:*

> *but the upright shall have good things in posses-*
> *sion.* Proverbs 28:10

If you are one of *"the upright,"* this promise is yours. YOU *"shall have good things in possession."* That is God's unfailing promise.

- 10 -

The Power of the Tongue

Death and life are in the power of the tongue:
and they that love it shall eat the fruit thereof.
                                    Proverbs 18:21

"Death and life are in the power of the tongue." That's a lot of power — more than many of us are willing to realize. What we say matters. We have the ability to speak either death or life into existing situations, both in our own lives and in the lives of others around us.

Don't be deceived by some of the extreme teachings on this subject. We cannot manipulate God. We cannot fill our lives with riches and ease and leisure simply by speaking it forth. We must, first of all, speak what God wants spoken. Many do not receive what they speak because they *"ask amiss"*:

Ye ask, and receive not, because ye ask amiss,
that ye may consume it upon your lusts.

James 4:3

Still, what we speak has power. If you constantly speak sickness, it will come to you. If you regularly speak health and blessing, that is what you will receive. Your words have the power to position you to receive either blessing or cursing. As you speak the blessing and promises of God, your soul begins to lay hold of that word in faith, and your spirit is able to receive the blessing from God.

Speaking forth the promises of God will build your faith and allow you to more fully trust in God, to rest in His hands and to give Him every situation of your lives. Only He can handle them properly, anyway.

Because our words have power, we must guard them, being careful of what we say.

The words of a man's mouth are as deep waters,
and the wellspring of wisdom as a flowing brook.

Proverbs 18:4

Sometimes, it's just better to be quiet. *As long as I'm talking, I'm not learning anything.* We must not talk merely for the sake of talking and, more importantly, we must still ourselves to hear God's voice. If we can learn to listen to Him, then our words will be flavored with His thoughts.

There is another reason for not talking sometimes. We must become good listeners as well as good speakers. When you speak, you expect others to listen, and when others speak, they want you to listen to them and want to feel that you really hear what they are saying. We can minister to people's needs in a greater measure if we are willing to listen carefully to them.

We may not always understand what we are hearing, but if we ask God will give us understanding of what people share with us. The words themselves are not always the important thing. There is a deeper level. When people begin to talk to you about their problems, they may speak very superficially about things that are not painful. It's very difficult for them to speak of things that are hurtful.

I spent four years going to psychiatrists, and I found that it was very painful to speak of certain areas of my life. So when someone is speaking to us on this level, we must be sensitive to their needs and their feelings. Ask God to give you grace and compassion, and knowledge as well, that you will be able to get beyond the surface problems and address the root issues. The roots of people's problems often run deep, but it is when we reach down to the root of the problem that we can minister to their real needs. God will help us to do it – if we are willing to listen well.

We must not only listen to what people are telling

us, but we must, most importantly, listen to what
God is saying about the situation. As a person is
speaking, God can be giving us instructions about
how we can minister to him. If we are just waiting
until the other is finished speaking so that we can
give our brilliant, prepared and rehearsed answers,
then we're not really listening. And people will
know it and close up. Why should they bother to tell
you about their situation if all you want to do is to try
to impress them with your knowledge?

Our knowledge isn't important in these situations.
Only God has the answers to deep problems. Only
He knows what to do with the roots once they are
uncovered. And often He can see in what direction
the roots stretch. Look to Him to show you the real
problems:

> *The heart of the righteous studieth to answer:*
> *but the mouth of the wicked poureth out evil*
> *things.*   Proverbs 15:28

When someone comes to you for advice, it is better
to listen, to pray, and to seek God's wisdom before
you respond quickly with an answer. What seems to
be reasonable to you may not necessarily agree with
the Word of God or with the need of the moment.
What people need is not just another opinion. Even
mature spiritual men and women sometimes give

natural answers, especially if they have responded quickly, but we can't afford to do it. This is a very serious issue, and people's lives are at stake.

"The heart of the righteous studieth to answer." Search out the Scriptures, seek the Lord and answer in the Spirit.

Foolish words do much harm, and Proverbs has much to say about those whose words are foolish:

> *The heart of him that hath understanding seeketh knowledge: but the mouth of fools feedeth on foolishness.*   Proverbs 15:14

> *A fool uttereth all his mind: but a wise man keepeth it in till afterwards.*   Proverbs 29:11

Most of us are not very wise in this regard. We speak too quickly and are later sorry, after we have said the wrong thing at the wrong time or to the wrong person. Since we cannot take our words back, we are left with the consequences. How much better it would be to *"keep it in,"* at least for a time. Then, even if we are foolish in our opinions, that fact won't be known:

> *Even a fool, when he holdeth his peace, is counted wise: and he that shutteth his lips is esteemed a man of understanding.*
> Proverbs 17:28

What a gem of wisdom this is! As someone once said, "It's better to keep your mouth shut and let people think you're wise than to open your mouth and erase all doubt."

> *A fool's mouth is his destruction, and his lips are the snare of his soul.* Proverbs 18:7

Don't let your own words destroy you. Be a person who speaks peace and blessing and the Word of the Lord. Let your words mark you as one who fears the Lord and seeks Him.

> *He that keepeth his mouth keepeth his life: but he that openeth wide his lips shall have destruction.*
> Proverbs 13:3

Guard your lips. Be careful of what you say. In this way you will *"keep your life."* This goes far deeper than simply not saying things we shouldn't. We must purify our minds as well, because what we speak comes *"of the heart"*:

> *A good man out of the good treasure of his heart bringeth forth that which is good; and an evil man out of the evil treasure of his heart bringeth forth that which is evil: for of the abundance of the heart his mouth speaketh.* Luke 6:45

One way to walk in purity in this regard is to walk in truth. Proverbs has much to say about lies and those who speak them:

> *He that speaketh truth sheweth forth righteousness: but a false witness deceit.*
>
> Proverbs 12:17

The world's ways are those of evil, darkness, and deceit. The righteous, however, spread light and truth. We must speak truth, no matter what it may cost us at the time. We must speak truth in every situation. If this is your stance, God will honor you for it:

> *A false witness shall not be unpunished, and he that speaketh lies shall not escape.*
>
> Proverbs 19:5

> *Lying lips are abomination to the LORD: but they that deal truly are His delight.*
>
> Proverbs 12: 22

These are strong warnings. God is greatly displeased with lies. If we want the Lord to delight in us, we must *"deal truly."*

Another misuse of the tongue is for gossip and slander and Proverbs focuses on these problems as well.

> *A froward man soweth strife: and a whisperer*
> *separateth chief friends.*   Proverbs 16:28

How may times have we heard someone say, "I really shouldn't be telling you this, and don't you dare tell another soul, but ..." And the damage is done.

A *"whisperer"* can split churches. A *"whisperer"* can do serious damage to a person's soul. A *"whisperer"* can do irreparable damage to a marriage. A *"whisperer"* can even *"separate chief friends."* Gossip is a very destructive force. May God have mercy on all gossipers! Their words are more destructive than swords, and they are akin to murderers. They don't just take the physical lives of their victims, however, they even destroy characters. Even if they later realize their error and ask forgiveness, the damage is done.

Flattery is another dangerous sin of the tongue:

> *A man that flattereth his neighbour spreadeth a*
> *net for his feet.*   Proverbs 29:5

Flattery is a *"net"* for one's feet. Flatterers say what they think people want to hear, not what people need to hear and not necessarily what is true. Flattery often involves lying (or at least exaggerating) and serves to give the hearer an inflated opinion of himself, rather than lifting up Jesus. The next time you hear someone complimenting you at length, consider his motives.

The tongue has the power to stir up strife and contention:

> *Where no wood is, there the fire goeth out: so where there is no talebearer, the strife ceaseth. As coals are to burning coals, and wood to fire; so is a contentious man to kindle strife.*
>
> Proverbs 26:20-21

What could be easier to understand?

As Christians, we are to bring reconciliation to those around us, not strife; and the first place to begin is by guarding our words.

We sin so often with our words:

> *In the multitude of words there wanteth not sin: but he that refraineth his lips is wise. The tongue of the just is as choice silver.*
>
> Proverbs 10:19-20

The tongue can be misused in so many ways. Lying, gossiping, slandering, flattering, speaking evil. The wise will guard their words. Some people need to take a vow of silence. Everything they say gets them in trouble. This should not be said of believers,

for God said, *"The tongue of the just is as choice silver."*
God can take that part of our body which James described as *"a fire, a world of iniquity"* (James 3:6) and
redeem it. The tongue of the just becomes *"as choice
silver."* It speaks words of encouragement and blessing, comfort and counsel. Each of us must allow the
Lord to use us this way.

And don't sin against your brother by repeating
something you have been told in confidence:

> *He that covereth a transgression seeketh love;
> but he that repeateth a matter separateth very
> friends.*   Proverbs 17:9

We must prove ourselves trustworthy. When
someone comes to speak with you concerning personal matters, keep that knowledge to yourself. If
people know that when they tell us something personal or intimate it won't be repeated, they will trust
us, and God will trust us. He will bring people for us
to care for if we have a mind to seek His responses, to
answer in love, and to keep our mouths from repeating anything of what we have learned in confidence.

Learn to speak *"a good word"*:

> *Heaviness in the heart of man maketh it stoop:
> but a good word maketh it glad.*
>   Proverbs 12:25

We have all felt burdened down at one time or another, only to have someone speak a word or phrase that instantly lifted us up. Isn't it amazing how "a good word" can turn things around so quickly? We can each have that same effect on others if we allow our words to be a blessing and a ministry to others.

> *A word fitly spoken is like apples of gold in pictures of silver.* Proverbs 25:11

What a beautiful word picture! In all situations, let us be those whose words are fit, speaking blessing and grace to those who hear. Let us allow our words to be used of the Lord, whether in encouragement, admonition, correction, or praise. This is clearly God's will for each of our lives.

- 11 -

Learning to Avoid Anger

He that is slow to wrath is of great understanding: but he that is hasty of spirit exalteth folly.
Proverbs 14:29

Let us pray that we may be those who will be *"slow to wrath."* We all need God's help in this area. Certain situations make us angry and bring us frustration, but the things that should really make us angry are the evil works the devil is doing: the sickness that he brings upon people's bodies, the famine he brings upon the land, the violence we see all around us, the children who are born addicted to drugs. Those are the kinds of things we should be angry about, not the frivolous things we all too often allow to disturb our spirits.

We should not become angry with one another. Instead, we should ask God to give us His grace, that we will not entertain attitudes of anger and wrath. We know that the fruit of the Spirit are just the opposite:

> *But the fruit of the Spirit is love, joy, peace, longsuffering, gentleness, goodness, faith, meekness, temperance ...*   Galatians 5:22-23

If we are living as Christ has set us free to live, our relationship with God will bear fruit in our lives. Others should be able to see the Lord's work in us. If we talk to people about being loving, merciful, and kind, we should not be growling, snapping, and arguing with them later. People around you are watching how you treat your husband or wife and how your treat your children. It is in this way that they judge the seriousness of your commitment to Christ and the depth of your spiritual experience. Your testimony will have a great impact when people see your life matching up with your words.

We all get irritated about one thing or another, and this is not pleasing to God. When we become angry with people, we are really getting angry with God. What we are really saying is that our way is better than His, and we are angry that things are not going as we had planned or wanted them to. Anger is often a form of selfishness.

Some of us get angry with God Himself, and that is

dangerous. "God, it's not fair," we say. "Don't You care, Lord, about what they are doing to me?"

Jesus' own disciples said such things to Him. One night when they set out in a boat to cross the Sea of Galilee and encountered a storm, they woke Him up and asked if He didn't care that they were about to perish. Jesus had been sleeping in the back of the boat, resting in the knowledge of the Father's care and protection. What a rude awakening!

Of course He cares! If He ever stopped caring, we would stop existing. Thank God that He cares and watches over us as a good Shepherd. He cares enough to allow those things we see as irritations to come into our lives. His purpose is not to make us angry; but He wants us to be polished gems, reflecting His light.

One way to shine brightly for the Lord is to resist the temptation to anger. Another is to learn to be peacemakers, those who turn away the anger of others. Proverbs assures us:

> *A soft answer turneth away wrath: but gᵣ ᵒus*
> *words stir up anger.*   Proverbs 15:1

If you want to argue, there will always be someone to argue with. If you want to start a fight, somebody's always ready for that. But if you want to walk in peace, it seems that's a much lonelier path.

"A soft answer turneth away wrath." God holds all the wisdom we need if we are to speak to people, to minister to them, to help them, to correct them without crushing their spirits. Our part is to come to Him, ready to learn from Him. As we live in the fear of the Lord, doing righteousness, studying the Word and working it out in our lives, we will mature in God. Part of that maturity is being able to hear Him in the situations we face daily and not to allow our spirits to become disturbed.

The Bible gives a wonderful example of a soft answer turning away wrath in Old Testament times. The Syrian military leader, Naaman, was a mighty man of valor through whom *the Lord had given deliverance unto Syria"* (2 Kings 5:1). He was highly respected, but he had a serous problem. He was leprous.

On one of their raids the Syrians had captured an Israeli girl, and she had become a maid to Naaman's wife. The girl now told her mistress about the power of God in the life of the prophet Elisha, who was in Samaria at the time. Eventually, Naaman was able to go to Elisha's house seeking healing for his leprosy. He went in faith, expecting to be healed. He also went in arrogance, expecting to receive the same signs of respect with which he was normally treated at home.

Elisha, however, failed to observe proper military

protocol. Instead of coming out to pay homage to his renowned guest, the prophet sent his servant out to him with a message. And it was an offensive message at that. Naaman was told to go and dip himself in the Jordan River seven times. His response was understandable:

> *But Naaman was wroth, and went away, and said, Behold, I thought, he surely will come out to me, and stand, and call on the name of the* Lord *his God, and strike his hand over the place, and recover the leper. Are not Abana and Pharpar, rivers of Damascus, better than all the waters of Israel? may I not wash in them, and be clean? So he turned and went away in a rage.*
> 2 Kings 5:11-12

Naaman was so offended by this breach of protocol and this infuriating message that he decided to go home without further contact with the Hebrews. Fortunately for him, however, he had servants who were both wise and humble:

> *And his servants came near, and spake unto him, and said, My father, if the prophet had bid thee do some great thing, wouldst thou not have done it? How much rather then, when he saith to thee, Wash, and be clean?* 2 Kings 5:13

It was true. Naaman had come loaded with gifts, prepared to pay a great price for the healing he needed. What could it possibly hurt to just try what the prophet was suggesting?

The soft answer of the servants persuaded Naaman. He did as the prophet had said, and not only was he immediately healed, he also became a believer in the God of the Hebrews.

Later, Naaman went back to see Elisha, who, this time, came out to meet him. The captain declared:

> *Behold, now I know that there is no God in all*
> *the earth, but in Israel.*   2 Kings 5:15

A soft answer had changed the situation entirely. Rather than inflaming Naaman's anger, the servants had turned it aside and brought healing and restoration. We can do the same. Why is it that we always want to answer back? Why do we always want to have the last word? God wants to put soft words in our mouths — for His glory.

It was good for Naaman to be surrounded by servants who spoke with humility and with soft words, rather than words that would further stir his anger. We need to be those whose words turn away anger.

There are some angry people we should avoid altogether:

> *Make no friendship with an angry man; and*

> *with a furious man thou shalt not go: Lest thou*
> *learn his ways, and get a snare to thy soul.*
>   Proverbs 22:24-25

"Angry! Furious!" You probably know that man.
And you are warned not to *"learn his ways."* Those
angry ways might become *"a snare to thy soul."* Let us
not have friendships with people who are habitually
angry. God knows best and there is great wisdom to
this command. If you stay around angry and dis-
gruntled people long enough, what they are saying
begins to sound logical. Their attitude gets into our
spirit, and we begin to agree with them. If you don't
want to become an "angry" person, stay away from
others who already are. Walk away from that situation.

The Scriptures repeatedly speak of the righteous as
being *"slow to anger"*:

> *A wrathful man stirreth up strife: but he that is*
> *SLOW TO ANGER appeaseth strife.*
>   Proverbs 15:18

> *He that is SLOW TO ANGER is better than the*
> *mighty; and he that ruleth his spirit than he that*
> *taketh a city.*   Proverbs 16:32

Men of *"discretion"* learn to control their anger:

*The discretion of a man deferreth his anger; and
it is his glory to pass over a transgression.*
                                            Proverbs 19:11

This reminds us of a passage in the New Testament:

*And above all things have fervent charity among
yourselves: for charity shall cover the multitude
of sins.*   1 Peter 4:8

Instead of anger, we are to respond to others in
love. As we love one another, we will *"cover"* each
other's sins instead of gossiping about them. We will
seek one another's repentance and restoration instead of looking for their downfall. It is our *"glory"* to
"pass over [cover] *a transgression."* Wouldn't you
rather walk in glory than to constantly bring others
to disgrace?

The person of *discretion* will *defer* or put off *his* anger. That means that he waits until he knows all the
facts of the case, until he has taken the time to pray
over the situation and give his anger to the Lord.
Being slow to anger is an indication of maturity and
of showing love to others. It is also a sign of wisdom.
Will you be *"slow to wrath"*?

Striving for Maturity

A good name is rather to be chosen than great
riches, and loving favour rather than silver and
gold.   Proverbs 22:1

We have purposely left until last one of the most
important subjects covered in Proverbs, our constant
struggle for spiritual maturity. Nothing could be
more important, and the book of Proverbs gives us
great insights not only in the need for maturity but in
the methods we must employ to achieve it.

The world, in its endless search for material
wealth, has great difficulty understanding the truth
of Proverbs 22:1. This is the hallmark of what God
expects of His people, *"a good name."*

"A good name," in this case, includes a good testimony, a proper representation of the Lord Jesus
Christ to the world around us. We are not just repre-

sentatives of our respective families, churches or organizations. We represent our Lord every day, wherever we happen to be, and we must be worthy representatives.

Because we represent Christ to the many who do not yet know Him, we have certain responsibilities. This knowledge should cause us to get serious about our role of ambassador for Christ in the world at large, to get serious about our work for Him. Let us serve Him well.

Taking one's responsibility seriously is one of the greatest marks of maturity. It means going beyond what I may want to do or what I may feel like doing at any given moment and, instead, doing what I know to be right, doing my duty. It means shouldering my responsibility without making excuses and explanations of why I cannot do what God has given me to do.

In a real way, the Book of Proverbs, which has been called a book of wisdom, is also a book of practical maturity. As we apply the lessons we learn from the voice of wisdom in this book, we grow in maturity.

One of the most fundamental ways we can grow in maturity is through prayer:

> *The sacrifice of the wicked is an abomination to the LORD: but the prayer of the upright is His delight.*   Proverbs 15:8

It is vain for the ungodly to go through the motions of religious observance. God doesn't even hear their prayers. He knows men's hearts. He knows the spirit of the words we speak. Therefore, it is not enough even to say the right words. God delights in the prayer of those who love Him genuinely.

That alone is reason enough to continue our prayer lives! When we come into the presence of the Lord, He is just as happy to be with us as we are to be with Him. When we bask in His presence, He is enjoying our company, too. He is delighted by our prayer. He is blessed by it. David prayed:

> *Bless the LORD, O my soul: and all that is within me, bless his holy name.* Psalms 103:1

When I delight the Lord, then He will pour out His blessings on me. I am blessed so that I can be a blessing. I first bless the Lord, then I bless others.

When we are babes in Christ, we can only think of coming to a church service to *receive* something from God. We don't consider the needs of others. After a while, although we still get blessings for ourselves in every service, we come into His presence to be *a blessing* to others as well.

When we are blessed of God we can carry that blessing into the streets and the inner cities and the nations to bless those who do not know Him. Then we become His arms extended. We become His mouthpiece. We become His hands, reaching out to the oppressed. What a privilege! Let us commit our works to the Lord, so they would work blessing to others:

> *Commit thy works unto the* Lord, *and thy thoughts shall be established.*   Proverbs 16:3

A person whose thoughts are *"established"* will do well in life. That's half the battle. Those who love the Lord have an added advantage in this area. They think holy thoughts. They even begin to think God's thoughts. His mind becomes part of our makeup. Paul wrote:

> *Be renewed in the spirit of your mind.*
> Ephesians 4:23

> *For who hath known the mind of the Lord, that he may instruct him? But we have the mind of Christ.*   1 Corinthians 2:16

The thoughts of the believer are positive thoughts. They are victorious thoughts, thoughts of wellness and healing. Believers are continually thinking of how they can bless, encourage, and help others.

One of the secrets of a godly thought life lies in

committing everything you have to God and in doing everything you do for Him. As the Scriptures declare:

> *And whatsoever ye do, do it heartily, as to the Lord, and not unto men.*   Colossians 3:23

There may well be, among the tasks required of us, some unpleasant ones. All of us are called on to do those sometimes. But if we can do even the unpleasant tasks *"as to the Lord,"* they become pleasant, and we can rejoice as we do them.

We are to praise God *"in all things."* If we will learn that secret, God will bless us through even the most difficult aspects of our duties to Him and to others. As you are going through the unpleasantness of being obedient in a task that does not appeal to you, know that you will not always be doing that task. If you are found faithful in the test, God will reward you mightily.

All of us would like to sit behind the desk of the bank president, signing checks and making important decisions. But you don't get to be president of the bank overnight. There are some lesser tasks to be performed first. As we grow, God can do more and more great things through us and in us.

You won't feel like obeying Him always. That happened to me in Australia once. I was to go to minister in Darwin, but on the way I had stopped at a Full Gospel Business Men's Convention in Tarwoomba, which is about eighty miles from Brisbane. The pastor from Darwin called to find out where I was. He said they were looking for me and were sorry I hadn't arrived there yet. I said, "Well, we're planning on coming. I told you we would be in the country by the 18th of October and we'd come up as quickly as we could. We've been invited to this Full Gospel Convention, so we'll be here for a few days."

As soon as I had hung up the phone, the Lord said, "I didn't tell you to come here. Get out of here today!"

He didn't have to tell me twice. I said, "Forgive me, Lord, and please help get me out of here." I needed a ride.

The convention was to continue for two or three more days. I asked everyone I could, "Is anybody going back to Brisbane? Have you heard of anyone going to Brisbane?"

Everyone seemed to be there for the duration of the convention, but when we got to the meeting that night, we were told that a brother had gotten a call from his family and had to return home to Brisbane that night. I knew that was an answer to prayer, and as soon as I heard it, I was on my way to find him and arrange for us to ride with him.

It is important to be where God wants you to be. It's also important to be there when He wants you to be there. He's always on time. He gives us the vision, and He gives us the provision to fulfill the vision. As we mature in God, we are better able to hear His voice and His direction. And, as we mature in God, we are also more likely to be faithful to heed Him. As Proverbs shows, it is not easy to find faithful people:

> *Most men will proclaim every one his own good-ness: but a faithful man who can find?*
>
> Proverbs 20:6

God Himself is looking for some faithful ones:

> *For the eyes of the LORD run to and fro through-out the whole earth, to shew himself strong in the behalf of them whose heart is perfect toward him.*　　　2 Chronicles 16:9

Tell God you want to be one of the faithful ones He needs. Let Him teach you and train you in faithful-ness and never be satisfied with just the appearance of usefulness:

> *Burning lips and a wicked heart are like a pot-sherd covered with silver dross.*
>
> Proverbs 26:23

A *"potsherd"* is a fragment of pottery — a small,

useless piece. It may look good on the outside, but it has lost its usefulness. The outside covering is deceiving.

Once you have made a decision to give your all to the Lord, never be guilty of looking back. Often, when we think of the things we have given up for Him, we remember the good times and not the bad, and we may begin to long again for those "good times." God is not only calling us to give up the things that displease Him, but to stop desiring them. We know that His way is best and we recognize the damage those things could eventually do to us. Thank God that we found His way.

Smoking is a good example of this. If you smoke, your mind may be on one of two things: either the temporary calming effect of the nicotine, or the future emphysema, heart trouble, lung or mouth cancer or other diseases that the smoking will eventually cause. If you remember only the "good" part of sin, you will fall in times of weakness. How can it be otherwise? This is why the Scriptures declare:

> *Wherefore let him that thinketh he standeth take*
> *heed lest he fall.*   1 Corinthians 10:12

Know why you stand in God so that you will not be tempted to go backward. And keep hungering after the Lord instead of looking back to the things you have left for Him:

The full soul loatheth an honeycomb; but to the hungry soul every bitter thing is sweet.

Proverbs 27:7

When you are hungry, everything is delicious. But when you are full, nothing tastes good. Hunger is essential to spiritual growth and maturity, and without hunger you won't get very far. If we are truly hungry for God, we will not be satisfied with anything less than His best.

Some people have all they can handle and are afraid to ask for more, for fear it will require too much of them. But if we are truly hungry, it doesn't matter what it costs us to gain more of God. When we are hungry, no price is too great to pay.

The Spirit of God is bringing us into all truth, but that doesn't come overnight. Truth is given to us step by step, line upon line, bit by bit. Don't be too proud to be taught. Don't be too wise to learn from others. Maturity includes being teachable, knowing that there is always more to learn.

The final chapter of Proverbs gives us a lovely picture of Christian maturity. The subject of Proverbs 31 is often called The Virtuous Woman. She is a pattern for believers who want to be walking in fullness in God. We see that she is a woman, not a girl, and she is a wife and mother, a position of responsibility.

The teachings of this chapter were given to King

Lemuel by his mother. First she addresses Lemuel himself, saying in part:

> *Open thy mouth, judge righteously, and plead the cause of the poor and needy.*
>
> Proverbs 31:9

Once, when we were traveling in Sao Paulo, Brazil, we met a lady who had a great burden for the poor and went out to minister to the residents of the most poverty-stricken areas of that city. The people had no protection against the elements and, when cold weather came, many of them died. They had no access to medical care. She was very greatly burdened for these people and did a wonderful work there.

The church this lady attended was probably the largest church in that area, with between eight hundred and a thousand members. I asked her if any of the people in the church went out to help her with her work among the poor. She answered that they didn't. They thought there were far too many poor people to be able to help them, so they didn't try.

God doesn't want us to give up, to look around us and say, "What's the use?" and just go home and forget the whole thing. We never know what good we might accomplish.

We must allow the Lord to lay His burdens upon us. We must open our mouths to judge righteously.

We must plead the cause of the poor and needy. This is pleasing to the Lord.

The virtuous woman did all this and more:

> *She will do him* [her husband] *good and not evil all the days of her life.*   Proverbs 31:12

God wants His people to do good to their spouses, to speak well of their family members and to lift them up before the Lord. When we have problems within the context of the family, we must take them to the Lord. We can speak of them to our pastors, if need be, but taking them to God is our first and most important obligation.

The virtuous woman has prepared wisely:

> *She is not afraid of the snow for her household: for all her household are clothed with scarlet. She maketh herself coverings of tapestry; her clothing is silk and purple.*   Proverbs 31:21-22

This godly woman takes care of the needs of her family. She gets up early (verse 15) and does whatever is necessary and so much more. She knows what is expected of her and she goes about her business in a way that is pleasing to God. She knows her duties and is faithful to perform them.

She also displays wisdom in her outward conduct:

She openeth her mouth with wisdom; and in her tongue is the law of kindness.   Proverbs 31:26

"She opens her mouth with wisdom." We all want to be like that. Since we haven't arrived, for the most part, we will not live in condemnation, but will continue to grow in the Lord and give Him full rein in our lives, allowing Him to make us more and more like Himself. We will let our words be those that please the Lord, bringing blessing, wisdom, instruction, correction, praise.

This woman is indeed blessed:

Favour is deceitful, and beauty is vain: but a woman that feareth the Lord, *she shall be praised.*   Proverbs 31:30

Be careful not to accept false praise. If God praises you, that's wonderful, but be careful when men do it. Sometimes the praise of men is a spiritual test. If you become puffed up because of being praised, then you have failed the test. Remain humble in the hand of the Lord. Your opportunities will come when God wants them to come, when you're better established in the Lord.

If you want to grow in God, then spend time in prayer. Seek His face. Listen to what He would say to you, and heed it. Be a man or woman of the Word.

Give yourself to grow in wisdom, in knowledge, and in the fear of the Lord. Trust in the Lord alone, and see what He will be faithful to do in your life.

We have seen the value of wisdom; we have tasted of the fear of the Lord. We have seen that we need to be teachable and to trust in God. And we are ready to continue growing in maturity. Now let us look at the voice of wisdom in the Book of Proverbs as it applies to our lives practically: How we view our children, how we handle money, how we deal with our anger. God's Word applies to our lives at the most basic levels, from understanding the nature of sinners to dealing with our own sin.

Let us determine to be those who live by the instruction of this marvelous book of Proverbs. The benefits will be not just to us, but to all those with whom we come in contact, and the results will be life-changing. The challenge is before you. You can do it. Come now, and feast on the wisdom of the Word of God.

Ministry address:

Dr. & Mrs. Jerry Kirchner
11352 Heflin Lane
Ashland, VA 23005